Praise for The Sale

"*The Sale* reminds us that doing business and living life with integrity is not just the right way, it's the only way. Well done!"

—Dave Ramsey, Bestselling author and radio host

"The principles in *The Sale* are more relevant than ever. Doing the right thing will never go out of style in life or business. I would highly recommend this book."

—Brock Bukowsky, Co-founder of Veterans United Home Loans

"Cultivating a culture of trust is essential for any business or team. *The Sale* is an excellent story that is relevant to any industry. The principles in this book are timeless!"

—Brad Harris, CEO of Dallas Jet International

"If you want to achieve ultimate success that lasts, *The Sale* is a must-read for every leader and their team. *The Sale* so powerfully captures how doing the right thing, even when it's the hard thing, is not only the key to true success, but the only path to fulfillment in both business and in life."

—Jamie Kern Lima,
New York Times* bestselling author, *Believe IT

"The best leaders bring others with them as they climb to the top of the mountain. Real success is not a destination; it's about the person you become on the journey and the choices you make to get there. *The Sale* beautifully explains these ideals and is the definitive blueprint on becoming someone worth following."

—Ed Mylett, Bestselling author of
The Power of One More

"What a great reminder that you really do reap what you sow. Doing the small, seemingly insignificant things the right way is the best path to success! I would definitely recommend this book!"

—Michael Porter Jr., NBA player

THE
SALE

a business fable

THE
SALE

The Number One Strategy
to Build Trust & Create Success

JON GORDON   ALEX DEMCZAK
Bestselling Author of *The Energy Bus*   Author of *Thrive U*

WILEY

Published by John Wiley & Sons, Inc., Hoboken, New Jersey.
Published simultaneously in Canada.

For general information on our other products and services or for technical support, please contact our Customer Care Department within the United States at (800) 762-2974, outside the United States at (317) 572-3993 or fax (317) 572-4002.

Wiley also publishes its books in a variety of electronic formats. Some content that appears in print may not be available in electronic formats. For more information about Wiley products, visit our web site at www.wiley.com.

Library of Congress Cataloging-in-Publication Data is Available:

ISBN 9781119762690 (cloth)
ISBN 9781119762683 (ePub)
ISBN 9781119762720 (ePDF)

COVER DESIGN: PAUL MCCARTHY
COVER ART: © SHUTTERSTOCK | KNIPS DESIGN

SKY10031966_030422

This book is dedicated to my loving wife, Erin, and to my sweet daughter, Kennedy. Thank you for always supporting me and for bringing out the best in me and others. —Alex

I dedicate this book to Alex for having the courage to tell this story, pursue your dream, and live the principles in this book. —Jon

Contents

Acknowledgments

Jon and Alex:

We are grateful for the many people in our lives who have modeled the principles in this book and have supported us in so many ways. We would like to thank the amazing team at Wiley, especially Shannon Vargo, Sally Baker, Michael Friedberg, and Deborah Schindlar.

Jon:

I am thankful to Alex for bringing me this great idea and story we could turn into a book and a powerful lesson the world needs to hear. I'm thankful to my family for their continued support and all the readers who continue to read and support my books. I couldn't do this without you and I really appreciate you.

Alex:

Thank you to my wife, Erin, for constantly bringing out the best in me and for encouraging me to pursue my dreams. Thank you to my parents, Carla and Basil, and to my sister, Morgan, for always being there for me and for living your lives with integrity. Thank you to all my extended family members for your constant support.

Thank you to my co-author, Jon Gordon, for being a mentor in my life and for encouraging me to step out of my comfort zone in faith.

Thank you to editor Nathan Hassall as well as Carla Demczak, Basil Demczak, Cindy McCachern, John McCachern, Joyce Cornwell, and Ron Cornwell for reviewing the manuscript of this book to make it the best it could be.

Thank you to my friends, family, mentors, and organizations who have encouraged me to be the best version of myself and who have been great examples of what it looks like to lead with integrity. You know who you are.

Most importantly, I would like to thank God for imprinting this story on my heart. The message of this book is one that must be told.

Introduction

Spend just a few minutes on social media and you will see a lie that is pervasive in our society. The lie says that your success, fame, and fortune are the most important things about you, and that you need to achieve those things, no matter the cost—even if it means compromising your morals, cheating the system, or hurting others in the process. Many people believe that pushing others to the side while elevating themselves in order to get ahead is just part of the process on the path to success.

But what if there was a better way? What if you could be wildly successful without sacrificing your soul? What if there was a secret to true and lasting success? We believe the secret can be found in a frequently overlooked and underutilized principle: integrity.

While it may seem counterintuitive, living with integrity and putting the needs of others above your own actually helps build trust and ultimately leads to your own success. Of course, you will need talent to succeed, but it is integrity and character that maximize your talent and lead to the fulfillment of your greatest potential.

Turn on the news and you'll often hear the stories of leaders who achieved the pinnacle of success in their careers, yet their lack of integrity brought everything crashing down around them. The ripple effect of their wrongdoing damaged the reputation of their organization, destroyed their credibility, and devastated relationships with the people they cared about most.

In our work with thousands of individuals, companies, professional sports teams, and schools, it has become clear that integrity has never been more important. So much is at stake, and so many things improve when you do things the right way over time—reputation, legacy, financial success, upward mobility at work, team unity, family, and relationships.

While this fable takes place in a business setting, the principles in this book can be applied to individuals, groups, or teams of all types.

As you read this story, we hope that you will be inspired to reflect deeply about your life, examine your character, and live your life with no regrets. We think you'll be glad you did.

Jon and Alex

Chapter 1

Matt's Crazy Life

Matt always woke up feeling anxious, and today was more of the same. He hopped out of bed when his alarm clock went off at the usual time of 5:30 a.m. As he got dressed, his wife, Kendra, rolled over in bed and asked, "How many days did you say you'll be gone this time?"

"Four days. It will go by quick," he said as he walked into the bathroom to brush his teeth. After fifteen years of marriage, Kendra was used to Matt's hectic work schedule and tried to make the most of her time when he was gone. She was thankful he made a great living, but deep down she had a feeling that their lifestyle was not sustainable and was not ideal for their two kids.

"Alright, be safe, honey," she said.

"Thank you. I'll make it back on time this time."

"Sure, we'll see about that," she said. Kendra knew Matt rarely made it back on time from his long road trips. She was starting to resent him and their marriage because of his physical and emotional distance. The previous year, Matt had been away for a total of 250 days. He saw himself as the provider and did whatever it took, including working long hours, to support his family.

Matt put on his suit, kissed Kendra goodbye, then went to the kids' rooms and told them he loved them. He closed their bedroom doors and left for another business trip.

This time the destination was Tokyo, Japan, to meet with his prospects about a new technology his aviation company, Turnbow Technologies, had developed. After college, Matt had started as an intern at Turnbow, the company his grandfather, Jerry Williams, started in the 1980s. Over the years, Turnbow had become one of the most successful aviation technology companies in the country, known for its outstanding service to clients, great company culture, and mission-oriented values. The company was regularly rated as one of the top American employers and best places to work. Thousands of people applied to work at Turnbow each year. Matt had always felt destined to work for the family business and never considered other career options.

Matt's older brother, Luke, graduated with an MBA from Harvard Business School. Luke and two of his friends started a company called Crypto-Magic, an innovative blockchain technology. A few years after starting the company, they sold it and made millions. Luke was set for life. Matt had always looked up to his older brother and yearned for the life he had. Recently, Matt had felt bombarded by the steady stream of pictures on social media, highlighting Luke's world travels with his wife and three kids in exotic locations where Matt wished he could take his family. Matt believed that if he could just make more money, he would have the level of flexibility and financial security that his brother had.

When Matt started with Turnbow, his goal was to make millions by his 30th birthday; but now he was 39, his marriage was struggling, he was rarely home, the big sale had eluded him, and he felt like he would never measure up to the picture of success he had created in his mind. To add insult to injury, most of the people he worked with didn't even like being around him. He came across as arrogant, and most people felt that he wasn't willing to talk to them unless he thought they could be useful to him in some way. Many employees in the company rolled their eyes at Matt's behaviors at work and avoided him whenever possible. Because

Matt's grandfather was the founder and CEO of Turnbow, no one was willing to call him out or hold him accountable for his actions. Even worse, they believed the only reason Matt still had a job at Turnbow was because he was Jerry's grandson. Matt truly loved his grandpa and was always on his best behavior when he was around him; but around other employees he was a different person.

Matt's fellow employees saw him as an ego-driven individual who took advantage of others and didn't live up to his commitments. At a recent work event at a local bar, Matt told his team he would pay for their tab. Toward the end of the night, Matt announced that he had to get home to his kids and left without paying the bill, and no one was even surprised. The minute he left, the team seized the opportunity to complain about him and express their mutual disdain. Matt always tended to say one thing but do something else. Although he was competent in his job, his lack of character had seeped into many areas of his life. He fell short of every standard and principle that Turnbow was built on.

Matt knew deep down that things were not okay, but he had no idea how to rectify his situation. He was blind to his own actions and was unaware of the ripple effect his lack of integrity was having on his work team and his family. They all knew that something had to change.

Chapter 2

The Company of the Century

From its humble beginnings, Jerry founded Turnbow Technologies with an intentional set of principles and values. He didn't see employees as a liability on the expense sheet. He saw them as an asset. He didn't just hire people; he invested in them. He encouraged his employees to weigh in and be part of the decision-making process and found that this led to greater buy-in and engagement. The more he cared about his people, the more they cared about their jobs and the company. Together they built a culture, a team, and a company that would improve the aviation industry and the world. As the company became successful, Jerry stayed true to his core values and beliefs and didn't waver, despite the company's extensive growth.

As Turnbow gained more recognition, everyone wanted to work for them. They were featured in magazines and on television, and a common theme prevailed—there was something different about this company. Jerry and Turnbow truly wanted what was best for others and didn't just focus on the bottom line. In the early stages of the company's formation, Jerry had to let a number of talented people go—even some close friends—because they lacked a key component that Jerry required of all of his employees; always produce results with integrity. Jerry was willing to take a chance on employees or promote individuals if he knew they had the integrity and character that aligned with the company's values.

Multiple companies in the aviation sales industry made headlines because of sub-standard parts they supplied to airlines and aviation dealers. These companies took short-cuts, sold inferior products, and failed to perform testing and certification to ensure the airworthiness of the parts.

But not Turnbow Technologies. Jerry wasn't someone who chased quick opportunities for money or personal gain. He maintained a long-term view of where the company was headed, and he believed that if each employee did the right thing with the right values and intentions, Turnbow would grow exponentially over time. He wanted his clients to come back to Turnbow again and again because of their great service and integrity. And they did.

Jerry had a simple philosophy when it came to bringing people onto his management team. He promoted and partnered with people who displayed a great attitude, whom he could trust to do their jobs right. Jerry was known for saying, "You only control two things in this life, your attitude and your effort."

On a major television talk show, the host said to Jerry, "So, you have created one of the most successful companies in your industry, thousands of people apply each year to work for you, and your company makes a difference in the community and in the world. What is the secret to your success?"

Jerry explained, "Well, at the end of the day, people and integrity come first. When you start a business, you must remember that character counts. While we are an aviation tech company that delivers high-quality parts and products, we are really in the integrity business." He took in a confident breath. "Every day, our goal is to deliver results with integrity and have a great time serving others. When you have that kind of daily focus, exceeding the expectations of those you serve, success will come. The reason our company has had success for decades is that we hire great people who truly love their jobs and love the people they serve. We invest in our employees and, in turn, they serve our clients." The audience broke out in applause. The public image was good.

Matt watched Jerry's television performance from his hotel room. He loved his grandpa and, as a kid, had always wanted to be like him. But as he got older, he often forgot the character lessons he'd learned from him. At times, Matt distanced himself from his brother, grandpa, and other members of his family because he felt inferior to them. He felt he didn't measure up. Matt had the natural talent to be a great leader, but his values and character didn't fit the company culture that his grandpa had worked so hard to create. Matt dreamed of having a more significant role at Turnbow someday, but everyone, including his grandpa, knew he could not be trusted in a leadership role. If no one wanted to be around him, how could he ever lead others and positively inspire thousands of employees at Turnbow? Matt kept his dream buried inside.

Chapter 3

The Future of Turnbow Technologies

Now in his early 80s, Jerry was regularly being told by his closest friends and advisors that he needed to start thinking about who would replace him as president and CEO when he was ready to retire. Jerry knew that the best thing for Turnbow was to have a succession plan in place, identifying a new CEO who could lead the company for years to come. The industry was evolving at a rapid pace, and cutting-edge leadership was imperative. Jerry insisted that he would be patient in finding the right person.

Jerry had always hoped that someone in his family would succeed him in running the business. His only child, Bruce, had been a local TV news host for 21 years and had no desire to join the family business. That left his two grandchildren, Luke and Matt. Luke had made all the money he could ever want and loved his life of freedom. He didn't desire the corporate life and was happily raising his kids in Florida.

Matt was his only other option, but Matt was not ready to be a leader. Over the years, Jerry had heard many worrisome stories about him. He loved his grandson and wanted to make sure that he had a good job at Turnbow, but for the sake of the employees and the company at large, Jerry recognized that Matt was not prepared for a leadership role, especially not one as vitally important as CEO.

Jerry gathered his leadership team and formed a search committee for his successor. He was adamant that the search could take as long as necessary to find just the right person. First, the committee decided to review external candidates before considering internal candidates. Jerry wanted to help facilitate a smooth transition with the future CEO. He wanted to find the right leader with a fresh and vibrant energy and ideas to move the company forward.

Since the beginning, Jerry was the smiling face of the organization. It was his leadership that had propelled it to local, national, and even worldwide impact, with his insistence on great customer service, impeccable products, attention to detail, and integrity. He always focused on doing little things to make his employees and team members feel valued. He would regularly send handwritten, personal notes to employees to recognize them individually and thank them for their hard work. Jerry walked the aisles of the production plant to make sure that frontline workers were doing well, and he personally called clients to thank them for their business. Jerry seemed like a grandpa to all because of the love and care he showed them.

Despite how open and available Jerry was, he did keep some secrets. He was experiencing a health challenge but had decided not to tell anyone at Turnbow other than his board of advisors. Fourteen years earlier, he had been diagnosed with cancer. After multiple rounds of chemotherapy, it was eradicated. However, doctors recently told him that it had returned.

Despite this difficult news, Jerry's attitude and life perspective remained unchanged. In college, he played football and was a middle linebacker. Even though he was charming off the field, on the field he was a warrior, and he approached life with this same spirit. Jerry was determined that cancer shouldn't change the way that he loved, served, and cared for others every day, so he figured that everyone was better off not knowing and worrying about the state of his health. Even though he didn't talk about it openly with employees, people started to notice his physical decline. His trusted friends and family knew that someday he would no longer have the capacity to lead, no matter how difficult it was to imagine Turnbow without him.

Chapter 4

Stress at Home, Work, and Life

Matt and Kendra met during their junior year of college. Kendra was a cheerleader for the football team and Matt was a point guard on the basketball team. A mutual friend introduced them and they hit it off immediately. While they were dating in college, Matt always talked about the life that they could create together. Matt was a big dreamer and envisioned great possibilities for their future. When he put his mind to something, he would work to achieve it no matter what stood in his way. Kendra loved that about him and knew he was the one that she wanted to spend her life with after their first date!

Yet almost two decades later, they found themselves with unfulfilled dreams and an unhappy marriage. Over time, Kendra noticed gradual changes in Matt and the way he treated her and their two kids, Nick and Kennedy. Since the early days of their marriage, Matt would tell Kendra he loved her as soon as he walked through the door. But now, she couldn't recall the last time that had happened. He'd always been great with the kids and played with them whenever he was home. Nowadays, he was short-tempered, less affectionate, and found it difficult to keep up with the kids' energy, as his work fatigue got worse. He hadn't taken any real time off in several years. When Kendra asked him about going on vacation, Matt revealed his true priorities.

"We've been talking about going on a vacation as a family for over two years. When are you going to give yourself a break, so we can enjoy some family time?" Kendra asked.

"You know I would love to," replied Matt. "I am just so close to making a big sale. Maybe when things slow down at work we can get that on the calendar." Kendra rolled her eyes at yet another excuse from Matt. He always talked a big game, saying that his priorities were his faith first, then his family, and then his job, but this clearly wasn't true. Matt was rarely home and his family felt as though they were more of an afterthought than a priority. He had no idea the negative impact this was having on his wife and kids. Over the years, one of Matt's favorite pastimes had been playing catch with his son, Nick. Of course, it had been a long time since he'd made time to connect with him in this way, and suddenly, Nick was a freshman in high school.

Nick was excited to play high school baseball and couldn't wait for his first game. He had worked hard all summer and winter break to refine his skills and was ready to show what he could do. The week of his big game, Matt happened to be at home. He and Nick ended up in the backyard playing catch. Matt threw the ball to Nick, who caught it, and then looked down tentatively. "Will you be there for my first game on Friday?" asked Nick. "We're playing the Pleasant Plains Cardinals. They're really good."

"I wouldn't miss that game for the world!" Matt responded. "It's already on my calendar and I can't wait to watch you hit a home run!" Although Nick was nervous about his first game, he was glad that he had his dad's support.

After dinner, Kendra leaned over to Matt and said, "Nick said that you'd be at his game on Friday." She shook her head, already knowing he'd respond inadequately to her next question. "Is that true?"

Matt circled his fork around an empty plate. "I am going to try my best to make it, but I have a meeting with a client earlier that day in Toronto."

Kendra raised her voice. "Why did you tell him that you wouldn't miss it for the world? He's counting on you being there!"

"I promise, I will try my best to make it," Matt said as Kendra left the kitchen.

Friday rolled around and Nick's heart almost burst through his chest with excitement. At school, all his friends were nervous and excited for the first game of the year. There would be a tailgate party after the game, put on by all of the players' parents to kick off the new season.

Two hours before the game, Kendra was in the kitchen finishing up food preparation for the celebration when she got a call from Matt. She could almost mouth what he was going to say as he said it. "I am so sorry. My meeting went longer than expected and this is a really big client. I couldn't leave early."

A vein appeared on Kendra's forehead. "You promised your son you would be at his first game! He's talked about it for months! You knew the date!"

"I know, I'm sorry. My meeting today was really important," said Matt.

"More important than your son? Don't say 'sorry' to me, say it to him!" Kendra hung up.

As Nick walked up to the plate for his first at-bat of the season, he went through his routine. He looked at the left foul pole where his family usually sat for games, then approached

Stress at Home, Work, and Life

the plate. As he stepped into the batter's box, he noticed that his dad wasn't there with the rest of his family. His heart sank. He struck out on three straight pitches. He went back to the dugout with his eyes to the ground and threw down his bat in frustration. Nick ended up going 0–4 in the game without a single hit. His team lost 8–2.

At the post-game tailgate, Nick didn't say much. His phone rang, and he pulled it out from his pocket. It was his dad. He ignored the call, put his phone on silent, then put it in his bag.

In the car on the way home, Kendra said to Nick, "Honey, I'm sorry how the game went, and I know your dad wanted to be there to watch you."

Fighting back tears, Nick responded, "He didn't want to be there enough. He never comes to anything. I don't even care anymore. . . ."

Matt flew back home late that night and got in at 2 a.m. He was thinking about all the questions he wanted to ask Nick about the game, believing his son would understand why he couldn't be there. While taking off his shoes, he woke Kendra up. She shot straight up as if she hadn't been asleep.

"Why can't you at least have the decency to tell your son when you're going to miss his game? You told him you would make it and he trusted you! All the dads were there. Except you. Why do you care so much about money?" Kendra asked.

"Look, because of my great income, you have the flexibility to stay home and raise the kids, I thought that's what you wanted!" Matt wrestled the shoe off his other foot.

The Sale

"I didn't plan on raising our children alone," Kendra sighed. "You are absent from the kids' lives. I need you to provide for us more than just financially. I need you to be there for our family." She choked up. "If we keep living like this, you're going to wake up and realize that they're grown and gone and you'll regret that you missed out on these important moments. And you'll wonder why they want nothing to do with you."

Matt stood there, confused, as Kendra continued. "You seriously need to evaluate the person you've become, because you are not the person I married." Kendra shook her head as tears streamed down her cheeks. "This is not what I signed up for. We can't take this anymore, Matt! You need to wake up and things need to change. If not, then I'm done! I'll file for divorce!"

Kendra stormed out of the room. Matt swallowed the word "divorce." He was stunned. In his mind, he was providing financially better than most of the other dads he knew. Some months, he brought home more money than most people bring home in a year. Although the large monthly paychecks gave him pride, they also chained him to his work. Most of the pressure he faced from work was self-inflicted; he wanted to be the best at his job and make the most money possible. To make this happen, he worked late hours and made extra sales in order to achieve his goals. But deep down, it was actually Matt's feelings of inadequacy that drove him to work harder and longer to get ahead at all costs. He thought he was doing everything he could to provide for his family. If anything, he thought that Kendra should be more grateful for the job he was doing as the provider of their family. He didn't want to miss his son's baseball games. He believed he was the one making most of the sacrifices in the marriage.

Matt got into bed, and shortly after, Kendra did as well. Matt tentatively tried to rub Kendra's back, but she swatted his hand away. They didn't say another word to each other as they fell asleep.

Chapter 5

Mandatory Vacation

Jerry walked briskly into Matt's office. "Things need to change," he demanded.

Matt recoiled in his chair. He hadn't heard his grandpa raise his voice in years.

Jerry waved his hand in Matt's face. "You can't keep living like this. You need to take some time off work so that you can focus on your family."

Matt stiffened in his seat and shuffled some papers. "Why are you saying this? I'm having one of my best quarters and I'm just about to make a huge sale!"

Jerry shook his head. "You missed Nick's first game of the season after promising him you'd be there. Work is important, but not at the cost of your family. I didn't know how to explain to Kendra that you weren't there because you were working for my company! Your son needs you and your family needs you. You can't work 24/7."

Matt bit into the back of a pen. People weren't usually this forthright with him, but his grandpa had no qualms telling him the truth.

"If you don't change," Jerry continued, "you're done in this role." He stared Matt down. "I can't sit back and watch my grandson put his work over his family at my own company. How will I sleep at night with that hanging over my head?"

Matt put his pen back on the desk. "Wait. . .are you threatening to fire me?"

Jerry took a deep breath. "No. I just want you to take a step back and some time off. You need to get back to what really matters. It will be better for you, your family, and our company. Take a week off. I'm sending you and your family to California."

Mandatory Vacation

"I can't take that much time off during this busy season. Also, Nick can't miss a week during his baseball season. . . ."

Jerry cut him off. "I talked to Nick's coach and explained the situation. Nick will only miss one game and your marriage and family are worth it. So we're all good there. Listen, when I originally started this company, I worked long hours and expected my employees to work harder because I wanted to see the company succeed. I didn't have healthy boundaries and those actions took a toll on my personal life." Matt nodded but wasn't convinced. Jerry continued, "You remind me a lot of myself when I was your age. I wanted so badly to succeed that I didn't create healthy boundaries in my work life. I don't want the same for you. As the founder of this company, I want my employees to have healthy lifestyles and boundaries around work. I especially want this for my own grandson."

After a long pause, Matt tried to think of an excuse for why he had been so absent from his family, but he respected his grandpa too much to make excuses and ignore his own behavior. "Is it really that obvious?" Matt asked.

"Yes, it is. I want you to be successful in your job but not at the expense of your own family." Jerry's eyebrows furrowed with concern. "I know you love your job and are good at it, but you need to scale back. There is more to life than making money and having success at work."

"But I really . . ."

Jerry spoke over him again. "Listen. You need to take a break so you can have some time with Kendra and the kids. I've already had my assistant arrange travel so you don't have to worry about figuring out flights or hotels. I'll send an email to your VP to make sure he covers your clients so you don't come back to an overload of work." Jerry took a step toward Matt and shook his finger in an I-know-best-I'm-your-grandpa way. "I'm not asking you to do this; I'm telling you to do this. You need to be with your family. They need you right now."

Matt's face relaxed and he took a deep breath. "Alright, I'll go. Kendra will be excited about this. We've been talking about a vacation for a long time. It's easy for me to have good intentions when it comes to balancing work and family and it just seems as if I can never get it right."

"Great. Enjoy California."

When Matt arrived home that evening, he told Kendra about the vacation. "Praise the Lord!" Kendra exclaimed. The next day, they started packing, and Matt anxiously thought of all the meetings he would miss. He hated the thought of missing work, but he didn't have a choice. Besides, his family needed him and the last thing he wanted was a divorce.

Chapter 6

A Chance Meeting

Matt loaded their belongings into the car with the hopes of having a memorable trip. Excitement set in as soon as he started the car and they headed to the airport. He was actually looking forward to some fun and relaxation. Kendra couldn't hide her smile, and the kids were joking in the back seat. Matt was a pro at navigating his way through airports, so this part of their trip would be a piece of cake.

After a smooth first leg of their flight, they sat at the gate waiting for their connecting flight to southern California. Matt saw a notification on his phone that their connecting flight was delayed due to weather conditions. Their plane wouldn't be leaving for at least two hours, so Matt went to grab some food for the kids. Whenever Matt was traveling through the airport, he always ate at Dillon's Pizza. They had the best pizza he'd ever eaten, and he was excited for his family to enjoy it.

Usually, Matt didn't engage in conversation at airports. He didn't like being bothered. He was always preoccupied thinking about his next destination and the business he'd attend to there. But today was different.

A Dillon's employee tapped him on the shoulder. "Hey, sir! I think you forgot something." Matt looked over to see a tall man holding his phone.

"Wow, you are a lifesaver! I appreciate it," Matt replied, taking it from him.

"Of course, no problem at all. Do you travel through this airport often?"

"Yes, I usually connect through here several times a month for work. This is a big airport! How long have you been working here?" Matt asked, trying to move the conversation along.

"I've worked here for about fifteen years. But the way I see it, I've never worked a day in my life!" He put his hand out, "Randy."

Matt lifted his hand to meet Randy's and they shared a strong handshake. "Matt. Nice to meet you." He put his hand back by his side and squinted his eyes. "What do you mean you've never worked a day in your life?"

Randy let out a confident laugh, "When you truly love what you do, it's not work. It's a calling. I know that I was put on this earth for this very reason."

"To wipe the tables at Dillon's Pizza?" Matt asked, feeling bad as he said it.

Randy smiled, "To meet people like you each day." Randy looked Matt up and down. "I do my work with purpose because it gives me life. Most people my age have already retired, but it seems to me, the ones who don't have a purpose don't have a real reason to live." Randy scratched his well-kept gray beard. "My team does what it can to take care of each traveler who comes through this airport every single day. We know that the small details make a big difference and our goal is to help you have a great experience while traveling, which can be stressful!"

Randy's response impressed Matt. "That's awesome. I wish I had your positive outlook about my job," he replied.

"Why don't you? Life's too short to do something you don't love. I didn't always love what I do every day. I cultivated a love for it over time."

Randy's direct question caught Matt off guard. He hesitated, and then rambled, "Well, I work at a great company, but I don't really feel like I make much of a difference.

I know I've made more enemies than friends at work. And I bring a lot of my work stress home. So things are pretty stressful there too." Matt couldn't believe he'd just revealed so much about his life to a complete stranger.

Randy nodded. "I would have guessed as much. But I also know you have more potential than you can possibly imagine." Randy took out a business card and handed it to Matt.

Unsure why an employee who was wiping tables had a business card, Matt took it and placed it in his wallet.

"We should grab a bite to eat next time you come through this airport. I'll get my team to cook you up one of our specialty pizzas. How about you call me next time you are connecting here?" said Randy.

"Sure," Matt said, certain that he would never see Randy again.

Chapter 7

The Trip

Matt and his family finally arrived in California. The kids were ecstatic. Nick seemed to have forgiven Matt for missing his game, and conversation between them flowed easily. As soon as they checked into the hotel, they all changed into their swimsuits and went straight to the beach. Matt's first order of business was hiring a surf instructor to help Nick learn to surf like he'd always wanted, and Kennedy spent a couple of hours crafting a six-foot sand sculpture with Kendra. After a full day at the beach, they enjoyed an elegant dinner overlooking the ocean. For once, the entire family was together at dinner with no distractions, just each other. Matt even left his phone in the hotel room, at Kendra's insistence.

It was a magical experience. They forgot their problems, fights, and issues. Through all the craziness and busyness as a family, they had become disconnected, and vacation was exactly what they needed to reconnect. Matt was finally able to relax and spend quality time with his wife and kids. Kendra caught glimpses of the man she married.

Getting away from the office was exactly what Matt needed. After a few days he could already feel the stress leaving his body and felt calm for the first time in a long while. He knew he should have planned a vacation like this sooner. He always talked about it and hoped it would happen, but he never acted. The whole family was excited despite the tension between them over the past few weeks.

The days flew by, and on the second-to-last day, the family walked barefoot on the beach. As the low-tide waves lapped against the shore, Kendra said to Matt, "I love you, Matt, but I wish it didn't take a family vacation to get you back."

"What do you mean?" asked Matt.

"Well, this has been such a great week and I feel like you've been so emotionally present with me and the kids." Kennedy and Nick listened to hear what their mom was saying. "But I'm nervous about what's going to happen when we get back home."

Kennedy ran over and hugged her dad. "I miss seeing you, Dad."

Matt addressed the family. "I'm sorry I've let you all down and haven't been there for you. I want to be a fully-present dad, not just a dad who makes money. I've been absent lately and want to make things right. I want to get better."

Kendra thanked Matt for his apology, but deep down she remained skeptical. She wouldn't believe it until she saw it. Matt had said this type of thing before.

Finally it was time to leave. The family packed their things into the rental car and headed to the airport. At their connecting airport they experienced another flight delay, this time due to a mechanical issue. Matt was annoyed, thinking about all he had to do to prepare for work when he got home, but he knew there was nothing they could do. As the family settled into the seats near their gate, Matt walked away to make a work call when someone tapped him on the shoulder.

"So good to see you, Matt!" Matt turned around to see the guy who had wiped down the tables at Dillon's. "How was your vacation?"

"It was excellent, thank you. Much needed. My family and I really enjoyed it." Matt wracked his brain to recall the guy's name.

"That's great to hear. I'm glad you were able to have some quality time with your family."

42

The Sale

"Yes, we all enjoyed it. We feel recharged," said Matt.

"That's great," the table wiper said again, as Matt spotted "Randy" on his name tag.

"I'll be connecting through here again on Thursday. Can we meet then?" Matt heard himself say this, but couldn't believe his ears. Had he just asked this table wiper from Dillon's to get together?

Randy checked the calendar on his phone. "That works just fine for me. Give me a call when you land and I'll make sure they have a specialty pizza in the oven for you." Randy smiled.

"I'm looking forward to it." Matt smiled back as he wondered how this was happening.

Although tired from the trip, Matt couldn't help but sense Randy's energy. He felt a genuine sincerity and connection with him, even though they had just met. They said their goodbyes, and Matt rejoined his family to wait for their flight to take off.

Upon returning home, the family could not stop telling stories and laughing about the fun times they had experienced on vacation. Matt cooked some steaks on the grill and the entire family watched a movie then played board games. Kendra felt so replenished after the trip and was excited that Matt seemed like himself again. There was a connection that they hadn't experienced in a long time. Kendra was hopeful, but scared of what would happen when Matt went back to work.

Chapter 8

The Big News

The next morning, Matt was back at work bright and early. One thing that was clear to him; his VP of Sales, Tony, was the same irritating guy he was when Matt left. Tony had been Matt's boss for a few years and knew a lot about the aviation industry. He took pride in his industry experience and regularly reminded Matt of all the ways that he lacked experience and could improve. Matt struggled to connect with Tony and their work relationship was strained.

"Close the door behind you. I have some big news," Tony said, as Matt followed the instructions and sat down, taking note of Tony's clean-shaven, smug face. "You'll never believe this. While you were gone, one of your biggest clients, Thrive Airlines, reached out."

"What?!" Matt responded, almost falling out of his seat.

"They wanted to follow up with you on the engines. They want to come in two weeks to see the engines in person." Matt's heart dropped. The engines were not yet ready for market.

"That's great news. . . ." Matt sighed. "But we still haven't received an 'all-clear' test rating for those engines yet. We might as well tell them to save their time, because they can't acquire them without the passed test."

Tony grinned widely. "I haven't told you the great news yet." He paused for dramatic effect, looked down at Matt, and changed the pitch of his voice. "Let's just say . . . I know a few people over at the inspection office. I made a few phone calls and we're all set."

"Wait, what? So they're all good to go?" Matt asked. "I can't believe all this happened while I was gone!"

"Well, they're not necessarily ready to go, but the inspection reports now *say* that they're ready to go." Tony winked.

Matt's lips flatlined and his eyebrows dipped. "Wait . . . the engines have not actually cleared inspection, but we received a certificate saying that they passed?"

"Yes, sir!" Tony replied strongly. "We can now sell them."

"Wow," Matt replied, lost for words.

"Is that all you got? 'Wow'? This sale could be life changing for you, me, and the entire company. If Thrive Airlines buys our engines for their fleet, this will be the biggest sale in company history!" Matt already knew the implications of this sale. It would bring Turnbow around seventy-two million dollars in revenue, and Matt alone would get a gross commission of $7 million. This type of sales opportunity generally comes around only once in a lifetime. Matt's mind raced. This would be his big break. He could escape the rat race. He could spend more time with his family. He would finally be on par with his brother. He thought about how proud Jerry would be. But he also wondered what would happen if he found out they agreed to sell the engines to a client knowing that the complete protocol had not been followed.

"Surely my own grandpa wouldn't be that upset. I mean, I would be bringing in seventy-two million dollars for the company. He wouldn't be mad at me, right?"

Tony shook his head. "Of course not. Jerry is an amazing guy, one of the best around, but at the end of the day, he's a businessman just like you and me. He wouldn't want us to pass up an opportunity as good as this."

Matt had spent the entirety of his professional career trying to position himself to make a sale of this magnitude. Thrive Airlines was excited about buying the engines because it would mean significant fuel efficiency for their planes. The company was a major player in the airline industry and the new engines Turnbow had created were cutting edge. Yet Matt didn't feel good about making a big decision like this without the counsel of his grandfather. Matt knew that Jerry was one of the most forthright and honorable men he had ever knew. If Matt told him about this, Jerry might say to wait until they got a passed test result and Matt might lose the deal. If he didn't tell him, he could always move forward with the sale and ask for forgiveness later.

Matt thought about his travel schedule and how much time he would be able to spend with family if he could just bring in more money. A $7 million commission check would change Matt's world and would allow him to retire early like his brother. With all that money, he wouldn't have to report to his controlling boss for every decision he makes. He could do his own thing, invest his money, live off the interest, and consult in his free time.

"You need to start preparing for Thrive Airlines," Tony said. "They'll be here in two weeks and we need to put on a great show. The information I shared with you can't leave this room. Understood?"

"Understood."

As Matt opened the door to leave, Tony yelled, "Have a great night, money bags!" Matt pretty much danced out of the room, knowing he was about to be set for life.

Chapter 9

The Four Laws

Although Matt wanted to be wealthy, an annoying voice in the back of his mind was telling him that making the sale in this way was wrong. Each morning leading up to the meeting with Thrive Airlines, he would flip-flop between excited and stressed out. He often struggled with anxiety, but this was a different kind of anxious, and he had never felt quite right since meeting with Tony.

Kendra noticed the change. During an early morning breakfast, she asked, "What's going on with you? We just got back from an amazing time in California."

"I'm just a bit stressed at work, that's all," Matt replied.

After a back-and-forth exchange that didn't really go anywhere, Kendra told Matt he should see a doctor, and Matt decided to take her advice.

After a routine examination, the doctor explained to Matt that he was struggling from anxiety and showing signs of burnout. Kendra thought it was strange that Matt had these feelings so soon after their vacation, but she had no idea about the potential sale he was obsessing about. The doctor prescribed benzodiazepines for generalized anxiety. However, since Matt usually tried to take as little medication as possible, he never picked up his prescription.

It was Thursday and Matt was flying home from a meeting. He arrived for his connecting flight earlier than expected. He waited around in the bookstore, flipping through a few business magazines while asking himself why he was meeting with a random Dillon's employee when he could be doing more important things like preparing for his big meeting. Still, he knew he couldn't turn down a few slices at

Dillion's! Matt wondered if Randy even had business experience. Either way, Matt had said that he would meet with him, so he felt compelled to stick to his word. He didn't want one more person to think he was a bad guy.

At 2 p.m. Matt walked over to Dillon's. From a distance he could see Randy talking with someone. Matt recognized that someone! It was Bill Troberski, president of the national retail company Vescoo. Matt didn't know Bill personally, but had read several *Forbes* articles about him and the billion-dollar company he had built. Matt was shocked to see him in person, and even more shocked to see him talking with Randy, as if they were great friends.

After they finished talking, Matt approached Randy, who stood up to shake his hand.

"Was that Bill Troberski?" Matt asked.

"It sure was!" Randy replied proudly.

"The same Bill Troberski who started a company from his garage that's now one of the top retailers in the country?"

"Yep. Bill and I have been meeting once a month for the past fifteen years, right here at Dillon's. I counsel him and help him apply the four laws," said Randy.

"Wait . . . that's crazy. How does he have time for that?"

"He makes the time. He's very intentional about it," Randy replied, clearly enjoying Matt's confusion. "Bill's secretary makes sure that he connects through this airport at least once a month so he can meet with me."

A waiter dropped a Dillion's pizza in front of Matt and Randy. Randy thanked him and offered Matt the first piece, putting it on his plate.

Matt squinted at Randy. Although he was looking at the man in front of him, he still didn't believe it. *What could Bill Troberski learn from this guy?* he thought.

Randy continued, "In the early stages of Bill's career, he only focused on himself and operated his businesses in a very selfish manner. It wasn't until his first two businesses failed that he hit rock bottom and started to consider the life he really wanted to live."

"Two?!"

"Yep. I met him right after his second business failed. I helped him through those challenges and we implemented the four laws. He now uses them as the pillars of his company," said Randy.

"So wait, you advise the famous president of a Fortune 500 company?" Matt asked, taking a bite into the soft, cheesy dough.

"I guess I do!" Randy laughed as his face wrinkled.

"Okay." Matt said, swallowing. "So what are the four laws?"

"You'll know soon enough," Randy replied, enjoying his new respect. Randy took one of the pizza slices.

"How can I learn about these principles?" asked Matt.

"I'll teach you. But like I tell everyone I meet with, not everyone chooses to apply them. I've taught them to many people who I never heard from again." Matt shuffled in his chair. He still wasn't sure whether to take the man seriously. "They're easy to understand but difficult to implement. They make you analyze your behaviors and be honest with yourself. It can be a scary process for some people."

Maybe Randy wasn't just a table wiper after all. "Most people blame others for their circumstances," he continued.

"They think the reason they fail is because of the government, their upbringing, race, educational background, or other outside factors. The truth is, the best leaders don't lead from the outside in, they lead from the inside out. People who blame others never reach their full potential. I try to help people realize their full potential. After many years of helping people with this, it's clear that only when they take full responsibility for their lives, including their actions, relationships, and personal integrity, will they start to see change happen."

"Wow, what you do sounds amazing!" Matt could hardly believe those words just came out of his mouth. He reached to take another slice, but his phone rang. It was Tony. Matt excused himself and took the call. "I need you to get back to HQ to get ready for the meeting with Thrive Airlines. I just booked you a flight that leaves in 20 minutes instead of the one you were on in two hours. Can you make the flight?"

"I'll try. I might have to run to the gate," Matt said.

"Good. See you soon. Why in the world were you on such a late flight anyway?" Tony asked as Matt hung up the phone.

Matt walked back over to Randy, hating to share the news. "Hey, I'm really sorry about this, but my boss just called and I have to catch a flight in a few minutes."

"One second," Randy said. He ran to the kitchen and came back with a box for Matt to carry the remaining pizza. "Here."

Matt took the box. "Thank you. I'll actually be coming back through next Thursday around lunchtime. Would you be available to meet then?"

Randy smiled. "Yes, I'll see you then. Bring a notebook."

Matt had to sprint through the airport, and made it to his gate just in time.

"It's your lucky day, sweetie. You made it by thirty seconds," the gate agent said to Matt.

Matt arrived back at Turnbow headquarters in time for a late meeting with Tony. Walking out of that meeting, he was frustrated because he had dropped everything to be there. The meeting mainly consisted of Tony boasting about how well he was doing and how much money he was going to make. Matt saw it as yet another example of Tony's controlling management style. There was no way he could work for this guy much longer.

Chapter 10

Law #1: Integrity Builds Trust

The following week, Matt landed at the airport and walked straight toward Dillon's. He saw Randy sitting at a table waiting for him.

"Thanks for rescheduling to this time," Matt said. "I'm so sorry I had to leave early from our meeting last week. My boss can be quite demanding."

"No problem," Randy replied with a smile. As he was talking, one of the employees brought over a specialty deep-dish pizza. Matt's eyes got big. "I enjoyed that last one so much! I can't wait to have some more!"

As they started to eat, Matt asked Randy, "So last week you talked about laws that you teach people in business. I want to learn more about that."

Randy replied, "Let's go. I'm ready to share. But you need to know, they aren't just about business. They have to do with who you are as a person."

Matt pulled his pen and paper out of his bag. He scribbled down the words that came so smoothly from Randy's mouth, even though it seemed like gibberish to him. "Integrity creates congruence, which builds trust. Without this first law, you'll never have success in any endeavor because people will not trust you. What type of business are you in?" Randy asked.

"I'm an aviation sales rep. I sell parts and engines for airplanes," Matt replied.

Randy shook his head. "Wrong. You're not in that business." Matt looked at the half-eaten pizza. He felt like he had just failed a test. "I'll ask you again," said Randy. "What business are you in?"

Matt tried to frame his next response a little differently. "I am in aviation sales. I know you've probably never heard of it but I work for a company my grandfather started called Turnbow Technologies. We're a huge company, with over 5,000 employees. . . ."

Randy interrupted, "You're missing the point. You are neither in sales nor aviation sales. . . . you are in the people business." Matt didn't really like that Randy was telling him what business he was in. Before he could protest, Randy continued, "As a sales rep, you provide people with what they want, and this provides your company with the revenue it needs to exist. No longer think of yourself as a sales rep; think of yourself as a 'people rep.' Every day, with a positive attitude, you deliver to people what they need and want and you do it the right way. You do it as a trusted advisor. You don't sell people things they don't want. You advise them and help them buy what they do want. Selling doesn't build trust. Advising builds trust. And when you say you will do something, you do it! The more you deliver on your promises, the more you build trust with others. Integrity works like this. When people see that your actions and your words align, they see the congruent behavior in your life and naturally want to follow you."

"Okay," Matt said, writing 'people rep' on his notepad, still not sold.

"Have you ever been around someone who says one thing and then does another?"

"Obviously," Matt rolled his eyes. "My boss is terrible. He constantly changes our commission structure and never follows through with anything."

"It seems pretty easy for you to point out someone who's not congruent," Randy said.

"I could come up with a lot more examples for you if I had more time. What's the next law?" asked Matt.

"Not too fast," replied Randy. "What about you?"

"What do you mean?" Matt sat upright.

"Would people say you're congruent? Would they say that your words and your actions align?"

"Yes, I'm a good person," said Matt.

"I didn't ask you that. I want to know if what you say and what you do match up."

Matt sat in silence and moved back in his chair. He put his fingers to his chin for about ten seconds. Randy nodded in encouragement, then Matt broke the silence. "Probably not. Uh, most definitely they do not."

"Why do you say that?" asked Randy.

"Well, if I'm being honest, my home life is a mess right now. Between you and me, my wife has mentioned that she won't be able to stay in our marriage if things don't change."

"Things like what?" Randy asked.

"Well . . ." Matt started, as he puffed his cheeks. "She says that I am not the same person she married fifteen years ago. It hurts to think that. But I have no idea what to do."

"Do you agree with your wife? Are you the person she married fifteen years ago?"

"Probably not," Matt replied in a monotone voice. "It's just that things are so busy these days and I can't make time for it all. I told my son I was going to be at his first baseball game and I missed it. I guess a person with integrity would have been there."

"You are correct," Randy said.

"My grandpa started a multimillion-dollar company, my older brother graduated from Harvard and sold his business right out of college and gets to travel the world with no financial worries, and everyone at work thinks I just have my position because my grandfather is the CEO of the company." Matt clenched his fists. "I know that people talk behind my back about how I don't deserve to be in this position. Someone accidentally forwarded me an email a few months ago saying how they could never trust me and how much of a jerk I am. I was outwardly mad and flipped out on them, but deep down, I couldn't blame them." Matt drew in a long breath, and exhaled slowly. "My career and life aren't going how I planned."

Randy blinked and nodded. He looked out the large airport windows, catching a glimpse of a moving plane, before looking back at Matt. "When we receive criticism of any kind, it's important to remember that even if it's only partially true, we can always learn from it. As hard as this is for you to hear, it sounds like you aren't demonstrating the characteristics of a person with integrity—at home or at work. Until you decide to live with integrity in your family and business, you'll continue to have these problems. You will always have to 'watch your back' and won't have full mental clarity."

Matt started doodling, but he was listening. He was too embarrassed to make eye contact as Randy continued, "You will be unable to fully focus on serving others because your mind will go back to the times you lacked integrity. No matter how much money you make or what success you have at work, these problems will always resurface. Instead of focusing on the job you have, you need to focus on the person you want to become. Are you ready to do that?"

"I think so." Matt looked at Randy.

"Good," Randy said, then resumed his lecture. "In business and in life, integrity is the cornerstone that creates congruence between what you say and what you do. If you tell your direct reports at work that everyone must show up for a mandatory meeting at 7 a.m. and you arrive 10 minutes late with no warning and have no valid excuse, you lose credibility and trust with your team. Similarly, if you tell your wife that you want to put your relationship with your family before your career but then you miss your daughter's birthday party because you're traveling for work, it's hard for your wife to believe what you're saying because your actions don't match."

Matt began to choke up, but he tried to hide the emotion as best as he could. He had ignored these issues for years, but he couldn't ignore them any longer. "Please, continue," he said.

"I want to tell you about an interesting study that a leadership expert named Dr. Ken Blanchard carried out. Blanchard set out to discover the top contributing factor to build trust within teams. How important do you think trust is?"

Now he was talking about studies? Matt was starting to get suspicious about who this guy really was. "It's very important," Matt replied coyly.

"Without trust, you can't build a successful team. Agreed?"

"Agreed," said Matt.

"Blanchard studied the interactions between team members to figure out the number one thing that held a team together and allowed them to trust one another. You might think that some of the factors would be discipline, hard work, friendship, or skills and abilities. Blanchard found, without a shadow of a doubt, that integrity was the number one factor for fostering trust in teams. By living with integrity, you give yourself an advantage at work and at home. Trust and integrity are the currency of great leadership and teamwork."

"I get it now." Matt said.

"Great," Randy replied. "Think about the game of football. There are eleven players on each side of the ball. Each individual player must trust that their teammates will carry out their responsibilities and stay true to their assignments. If just one person lacks integrity and navigates away from the game plan, it can result in a disastrous play. All eleven teammates must work in unison to accomplish the goal." Matt drew a football goal post and wrote "life goal" in it as Randy continued. "Over time, as a football team continuously practices, trust is built between the coaches and players and they all learn that they can count on each other to do their jobs. The same is true at work. If people at work don't see you living with integrity in all areas of life, it will be hard to build trust with them." Matt shook his wrist to alleviate the growing pain and carried on making notes, which were almost unintelligible. Randy said, "The same goes for your life at home. Integrity is not effective when it is partially displayed. People see through temporary, fake, or shallow behavior, and that's why it's so important to work on integrity in all the areas of your life. And here's the thing, no one is perfect.

I'm not. You're not. We all have our flaws, but the ability to have integrity while displaying humility and authenticity allows others to see who we really are. When we live that way, people are actually drawn to us because they know we are being true to who we are. They know they can trust us! Do you feel like you're the same person in all of the areas of your life?"

"Maybe . . . I've never really thought about that before," Matt answered, feeling a bit overwhelmed.

Randy took out a pen. "Can I borrow a sheet of paper?"

"Sure," Matt said, ripping a sheet off his pad. Randy drew a few circles and pushed it between him and Matt.

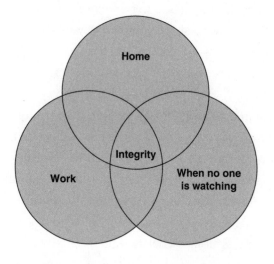

"This illustrates what I mean." Randy jabbed the paper. "Look at these three circles. You might assume that the way you act at work has little impact on your life at home with your family. These circles illustrate that this way of thinking is wrong. All of the circles touch each other." Randy leaned back and placed the tips of his fingers from both hands against each other. "What you do in one area affects the other areas of your life. It's easy to think that the decisions you make when no one else is around only impact you. But that's also false. Once again, those decisions touch your home life and all other aspects of your life."

Randy paused as Matt drew the circles himself and wrote, "My work affects my family." Randy took a breath and carried on, "Many struggling business owners come to me and wonder why they're failing and can't find success. I encourage them to find small wins in a certain area of their life. The reason for doing that is because, like the circles show, every area of your life impacts other areas of your life. When you decide to take ownership in one area, you slowly are able to win in other areas as well. When you look at these circles, can you see how the areas where you lack integrity rub off on other areas?"

Matt stared blankly as he ruminated on all three areas of his life before saying, "I don't think I'm congruent in all areas. But I can put on a show when I need to. And yes, I can see how my lack of integrity in one area rubs off on other areas."

"I never said this was going to be easy," Randy said. "Tony Dungy, the Hall of Fame football coach, said it best: 'Living with integrity is doing what is right versus what is convenient.' This definition is spot on. Often, living with integrity and doing the right thing is difficult. It's not always easy or convenient to live with integrity, but it's the right thing to do. Many times, the things in life that are easy to accomplish are not worth doing." Randy pointed behind Matt, who turned to see a line of people waiting for coffee. "Going with the crowd and fitting in is not what you're called to do as a leader. Making a difference in the lives of others often requires ignoring outside voices and doing the right thing, no matter the cost." Randy changed his tone. "Have you ever seen an orchestra play?"

Matt was caught off guard by the question and was beginning to lose focus. "Yes, actually. My daughter, Kennedy, plays the violin and is in the orchestra at her school." He tried to regain his focus and listen more intently.

"Great." Randy slapped his hands together. "Next time you're at one of her concerts, you'll notice one thing that you'll never forget about leadership. A person who leads the orchestra must turn his back to the crowd. While the people in the orchestra are facing the audience, the conductor must go against the crowd and face the people they lead. The same is true in leadership. There will be times when you're tested, and it will be convenient to do the popular thing or the expected thing. But the right thing may require you to go against the crowd."

Matt exhaled deeply after some noticeably shallow breathing. "Are you okay?" Randy asked.

"Yes, I'm fine. Just trying to process all this."

"I want you to work on applying this. Hearing about it is one thing, but acting on it takes it to the next level. When I asked if you could point out someone who lacked integrity, you easily pointed out that your VP does not follow through on his commitments. I have your first assignment. Before we meet next week, I want you to take some time to think about your own actions and complete this assignment." Randy handed Matt a notecard with a few questions.

Matt looked over the card, thanked Randy for taking the time to meet with him, scheduled another time to meet, and then headed off to catch his flight. Although his mind was on overload, he felt a sense of relief. It was hard to admit that he lacked integrity, but he felt relieved now that he had acknowledged this fact. For the first time, he realized that facing the truth is better than continuing to live a lie. A weight lifted from his shoulders. He felt strangely excited that he was dealing with these issues, but he knew it would be hard to write down his shortcomings in detail. Staying in his comfort zone was not getting him where he wanted to go and he knew it might be time to get uncomfortable.

While Matt was on the plane, he started to fill out the card.

The Card

- **Name a recent example of when your walk did not match your talk. Who was impacted by your actions?**

Matt's response:

- I am very bad about saying that I will be home for something for my kids or wife and then not following through. The final straw was missing Nick's baseball game for a work meeting that wasn't really important. I know I hurt my son's feelings when I did that and it has made things even worse between me and my wife.

- I recently invited the sales team to hang out after work and said "my treat," but then left early and didn't pay the bill.

- **Knowing that you lacked integrity in these areas, what must you do to make it right?**

Matt's response:

- Quote from Randy: "Your actions should speak so loudly that I can barely hear what you are saying." I now understand that I need to be more careful with the words I say and the promises I make. If I commit to something or someone, I need to make sure I follow through on my word. At home, I need to create small wins such as showing up early to the kid's events and asking how I can pitch in with Kendra around the house. At work, if I say "my treat," then I must pay the bill.

- **Who is someone you know who lives with integrity? What is different about them?**

Matt's response:

- I feel like, in the industry that I'm in, a lot of people don't live with integrity. However, I would say my grandpa does. He is someone who can always be counted on. It's clear that he models integrity in all areas of his life. The success of Turnbow is strongly correlated to his integrity, which he has implemented from the top down. My grandpa is always doing the little things right and I can't remember a time that I doubted his integrity or didn't trust him. He is intentional with his time and commitments.

- **At the end of your life, what do you want people to say about your character and integrity?**

Matt's response:

- This is a tough question that I have not thought much about before. But I guess I don't want my wife to be unhappy in our marriage because of my actions. And I think it would be sad for my kids to think that I don't care about them because I missed all of their important events in life. I also don't want to look back on my working career knowing that I had a huge platform to make a positive impact on other people's lives and I wasted it. I want people to say that they knew that I was there for them and they could count on me. I want people to say that when Matt said it, he did it.

Chapter 11

Growth

When Matt arrived home, Kendra was waiting at the front door, excited to see him.

"You look different today." Kendra threw her arms around Matt. "More positive. Who's the lucky woman you met?" she joked.

"You are," Matt laughed, pulling her in tight. "I met with this guy at the airport today and we had a long conversation. He helped me put some things into perspective and made me realize that I need to start doing things differently. We're going to meet sometimes when I travel through his airport. I think it will be very helpful."

"That's great!" Kendra said, giving a hopeful smile. "The kids and I just finished dinner. There's some food in there for you if you want. I need to help Kennedy with her homework. The dishwasher isn't working, so can you do the dishes? If you wash them, I'll put them away. Sound fair?"

"Sure," Matt replied with a grin as Kendra left the room. While Matt cleaned the dishes, he had time to think about all of the things Randy had told him. When he was done with the dishes, he went to his office and began writing. Matt figured he would only spend a few minutes working on this first assignment, but he stayed in his office for two hours. He realized he had never truly been honest with himself when it came to his actions and how they were impacting others. He teared up. He was finally acknowledging that he didn't have his life together. He had been so selfish with his family and the people at work. He felt overwhelmed as he thought about the negative ways he treated others. For the first time, Matt was ready for change.

After a long week of work, Matt was ready to meet with Randy again. Matt didn't bring his notecard. Instead, he brought six pages of notes filled with inspired thoughts. When Matt walked toward the restaurant, he saw that Randy was training a young man who looked like he was in high school. Matt sat near them and overheard Randy telling the young man how to properly wipe down the tables. Matt listened for about five minutes. He overheard Randy say, "It's about doing all the little things right. When you clean the tables and chairs, remember that people will use them to sit and eat. We want to make this the cleanest and most welcoming restaurant they have ever visited." After Randy finished talking to the young man, he walked over to Matt's table and sat down at 10:59 a.m., one minute before their planned meeting time.

"How was your first assignment?" Randy asked.

Matt replied after a deep breath. "It was good. I really needed this. Instead of just writing down a few things on a notecard, I wrote six pages of notes and examples of things that I want to change in my life. As you can tell, my life is pretty jacked up!" Matt laughed.

"You're doing great, Matt. You're right where you need to be," Randy said enthusiastically.

"I saw that you were training a new employee." Matt pointed at the boy who was cleaning a table on the other side of Dillon's.

"Yes, he just started working for us last week."

"That's great. What is your job title anyway? Are you a manager or trainer?" Matt asked, feeling bad that he had previously thought of him only as a table wiper.

Randy cracked his fingers and took a dramatic pause. "I have around 250 employees who work for me."

"WHAT?!" Matt exclaimed.

"My name is Randy Dillon. I started Dillon's Pizza twenty years ago. We have fifty locations around the country."

"No way! Wait . . . why are you dressed like a regular employee and wiping the tables?" asked Matt.

"This is what I am called to do. I am called to meet with people like you to help them become better leaders. I tried to retire, but after spending a month at the beach, I just couldn't handle it anymore. I knew I needed to have a purpose and a reason to wake up every morning. Coaching people like you is my purpose."

Matt was amazed. He couldn't believe that he had wrongly judged Randy. "I'm sorry," said Matt.

"Sorry for what?" Randy asked.

"Well, wrongly judging you. To be honest, because of how you dress, and after seeing you wiping down the tables, I still can't believe that you're the owner of Dillon's. I figured you were just an employee."

"No worries," said Randy. "But it's unimportant if I'm the person wiping down the tables or the owner of the company. That's why I dress as I do. I don't need people to know my role in this company or the success I've had. I want to build real relationships and friendships with people in my life. This is a great lesson for you to learn. You need to get to a point in your leadership where you treat the table wiper and the busboy the same way that you treat the manager and the CEO."

Matt was amazed. Randy truly cared about him and wanted to invest in his life. He didn't spend their time together boasting about his own accomplishments like many other successful businessmen. Instead, he was focused on asking Matt questions that helped him grow as a person.

"So, tell me about this past week's assignment," Randy said.

"Well, here it is," said Matt, handing the papers over.

Randy ran his eyes over it. "Wow. This is great," he said, nodding in approval. "I think you're ready."

"Aren't you going to read it all?" Matt asked.

"I will, after our meeting." remarked Randy.

"What am I ready for?" Matt asked.

"To make a change in your life. What you've written is clearly transparent. I think you're ready to start implementing integrity into every area of your life." Randy collected his thoughts for a moment and inhaled loudly. "The thing about integrity is that when your life is congruent, people trust you. Do you enjoy doing business with people you don't like or trust?"

"Not at all."

"Exactly." Randy pulled out a napkin and started writing on it. As he wrote, he said, "You see, I've actually created my own diagram for how this works. Many leaders keep this diagram on their desks because it's timeless. I call it the I-G continuum.

"Let me break down this diagram for you. Think about your business. You sell and promote products. You provide services for your clients. If you're a person who lives with integrity, people observe your actions. Even if there are days that you don't feel like doing the right thing, as people continue to see your commitment no matter how large or small the task, they take note of your character."

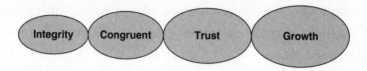

I-G Continuum

Matt took out his notepad again and wrote, "What happens over time is that the people around you become accustomed to your actions. They see congruence in your lifestyle. They see it in your career. They see it in the big and small things you do each day."

"Yes, this makes sense!" Matt said.

Randy continued, "When you model integrity in business, your fellow employees, managers, and clients conclude that you will be consistent and congruent in the way that you behave in other areas. Once you're known as a congruent person, people know that you're someone they can count on. Do you know what we call that?" Randy paused. "Trust. This is one of the most important factors in relationships, business, and life. When others can trust you, they not only expect you to follow through, but in many circumstances, they depend on you to follow through. Trust is something that is built through the first two stages of the continuum. Without trust, it's hard to have success in any endeavor. Close your eyes."

"Okay . . .," Matt responded apprehensively.

"I want you to think about someone you really trust. Someone you know would be there for you if you needed them. Think about someone who would drop everything they're doing to be there for you. What qualities do they have?"

Matt closed his eyes and took a few breaths. "Well, I can think of my grandpa. He is very dependable. As a kid, I was really into baseball. Even though my grandpa was more of a football fan, he knew it was important to me for him to be at my games. He would stand by the left-field fence near the foul pole at every game. During my first at-bat, I would always look over before I walked to the plate and would see him there. I could count on him to be there for me."

"Great example," Randy said.

Matt continued. "Also, I remember one time when I was younger, my grandpa took me to work with him for the day. He picked me up and we power-washed the company parking lot." Matt began to smile at the memory. "He's the CEO of the company and he was making sure that everything was clean and in order at 5 a.m. No one told him to do that. He just does things the right way and you can always count on him to make selfless decisions for the company. I will never forget that example of serving his employees when that wasn't part of his job description."

Randy was impressed. "Those are perfect examples. Your grandfather clearly has integrity. He has congruence. This builds trust and then people recognize him as a trustworthy person. And this leads to growth. In a business setting, growth can include revenue, profit, and influence. In life, growth would include emotional maturity, healthy relationships, spiritual growth, and psychological well-being. The bottom line is, if people can trust you and like being around you, they will want to do business with you. Integrity is truly one of the best-kept secrets in business. Most people think that you need a fancy degree, need to work overtime, or need to push others to the side to achieve success, but I'm here to tell you that focusing on integrity is the most important thing you can do for your life and your business."

Before they knew it, their time was up. Instead of the usual handshake, Matt gave Randy a hug. He couldn't wait to come back to see him again. After each meeting, Matt felt like he was becoming a better version of himself. Randy's lessons were timeless and life-changing. Never had Matt looked at himself and his actions with such honesty and introspection. He didn't know what the future would bring, but he felt more prepared to take it on. With each lesson he learned about integrity, he grew more uncomfortable with Tony's decision to sell the engines to Thrive Airlines.

Chapter 12

Law #2: Integrity Allows for Long-Term Success

Early the next week, Matt and Tony prepared for their big meeting with Thrive Airlines. As Tony continued to talk about how much money they would make, Matt kept thinking about his talks with Randy. In his heart, he knew they weren't acting with integrity, and yet he kept justifying in his mind why making the sale was the best thing to do. He knew he needed to talk to Randy again and went to see him on his next work trip.

Matt was intrigued by Randy, and even a little intimidated by his presence. "Tell me about your story," Matt probed.

"Ha!" Randy let out a booming laugh. "If only you knew my past. It truly is a miracle that I'm in the position I'm in today. The truth is, I have an addictive personality." Matt nodded; he had an inkling where this was going. "I was an alcoholic and addicted to all sorts of drugs. I was selfish and pushed away everything that was good in my life. I literally . . ." Randy choked up, ". . . lost everything. I began drinking heavily every day. Then, through the great gateway that alcohol can be, I began to use drugs."

"Wow, I had no idea," Matt said.

Randy wiped his eyes. "Those were my daily remedies for trying to cope with the stresses of life. I was only eighteen when my daughter was born. The responsibility of being a parent at such a young age scared me and so I ran. I left. I walked out on my baby daughter and my girlfriend." Randy placed his hands together and inhaled deeply to compose himself. "To this day, I have never even met my own daughter. I was so ashamed about my actions that I got into harder drugs. My addiction then led to gambling because I needed money for more drugs. I gambled away every penny in my bank account. I was homeless, sleeping on the side of the road and asking people for money. I was helpless."

"Seriously?" Matt couldn't believe it. "A homeless drug addict turned entrepreneur and business coach? That's such an amazing turnaround."

"Yes. When I was homeless, I only cared about myself. I did things according to my own schedule. I didn't care what other people thought. I only did what was easy. It was my way to escape the pain. One day, when I was on the side of the road, a man stopped to talk with me. He pulled out his wallet and grabbed a hundred-dollar bill. My eyes lit up because I knew I would be able to get my next fix with the money. But right before I grabbed it, he pulled it away and said, 'If I give you this, I get to spend a hundred minutes with you. Do we have a deal?'"

Randy broke into a smile—a small, lippy one, but a smile nonetheless. "No one had ever wanted to really talk with me before when I was on the street. They usually just gave me their spare change and moved on. I was homeless and didn't have a schedule, so I figured I would go to McDonald's with this guy so I could get some drug money. I was desperate." Fighting back tears, Randy went on. "The time we spent together at that McDonald's was life-changing. The man told me that even though I had made mistakes, I didn't have to live in the past. He helped me turn my life around. He shared how some of the past decisions he had made left him with regret."

Matt's eyes were wide and unblinking. He nodded to encourage the story to continue. Randy went on. "He told me that he wanted to help me avoid some of that pain. Despite me saying that I was a drug addict, had a gambling addiction, and left my family, he told me that I still had hope and a future. For years on the street, conversations rarely moved beyond surface-level. No one ever valued me the way that man did. At the end of our hundred minutes together, he gave me the money as promised. Every fiber in my body wanted to spend all that money on drugs. I was only two blocks away from my dealer and knew I could get a quick fix."

Randy's hands clenched. "But something felt . . . different." He pounded his chest in a rare glimpse of pride. "I couldn't believe it, but for the first time in many years, I saw my drug addiction from an outside perspective and it looked meaningless. That man connected me with the local church he attended and took me to an AA meeting the same day. I then got plugged into a ministry that helps former convicts and homeless people get jobs. And sure enough, two months later, I got my first job at an airport. I was tasked with wiping all of the tables in the airport food court. That's all I did. Every day I showed up at 4:30 a.m. to clock in, and made sure the restaurants were clean. It wasn't glamorous by any stretch, but I knew that if I wanted to grow, I needed to start somewhere. I cleaned and cleaned, met people, cleaned some more, and started to develop a way of living that I knew was best for me." Randy nodded and smiled. "Once I was back on my feet, I wanted to start my own restaurant to serve others, and the rest is history."

Matt shook his head. Tears welled up in his eyes. "How?" He coughed. "How did you turn your life around and become the person you are today? It's hard to believe your story looking at you now."

"I know it's hard to believe, but that's why I'm passionate about helping people like you realize the importance of making the most of your life. I want to help you have multidimensional success."

"What do you mean?" asked Matt.

"Well, when you have integrity in all areas, you allow yourself to have success in multiple areas of life. In your case, that is professionally and at home. I am filled with regret that I have a daughter who I have never met. Instead of being a father figure and raising her, I missed out. I want you to be successful at work, but I don't want you to sacrifice the joy of being with family in exchange for that success. Would your wife say that you provide?"

"I would say so," Matt said. "The past two months I've brought in two very large commission checks. Bigger than the amount the average person brings home in a year."

Randy blinked at Matt. Matt knew he saw right through him. "That's an issue. You need to be focused on providing for your family more than just financially. If you have integrity, you will be able to provide for your family and have success at work as well as at home. I watch families walk through this airport every day and see parents who are so consumed with their phones that it feels like their family is an afterthought. I don't want that for you." Matt smiled like a teenager who knew he'd been caught. Randy said, "I know you can and will have success at work and at home. I will regret that I left my girlfriend and child for the rest of my life. I can never take that back. But I can help you realize that you have been blessed, and beg you not to waste it. If you start living with integrity, you'll be able to have success in multiple areas of your life. You don't have to sacrifice one for the other."

Matt appreciated his time with Randy more and more. He knew that his family had tried to talk with him before about being more emotionally present, but he had never been able to implement this into his life long-term. He looked past Randy at the red wall.

"Matt," Randy said, getting his attention again. "My friend, Frank, built a very successful company that started in his living room. As they began having success, they made a commitment to do everything with integrity. They even made a list of everything that could derail them, for example, complacency, inaccurate reporting, theft, bad behavior, et cetera, and made a plan to put safeguards in place to protect themselves. Looking honestly at what can derail you will help you maintain your integrity. Frank's team knew how easy it would be to sacrifice integrity when trying to build a business, so they created standards to help them stay on track. This kept them focused on long-term success instead of short-term gains. This is really significant because integrity leads to long-term success. I have seen this over and over in my life and in the lives of the people I mentor."

Matt was attentive and took everything in. "Tell me more about that," he remarked.

Randy replied with a smile. "Many people you will encounter in business chase quick money. They don't realize the consequences of their decisions and they conduct their business in a short-sighted manner. Let me tell you a story about two executives I meet with once a month. They run a successful mortgage company together. The company employs over five thousand people and is consistently ranked as one of the top companies to work for in America. What is so impressive about them is that they consistently encourage their leadership team to make decisions that will help the company be profitable years from now."

Matt leaned in closer as Randy went on. "They make wise decisions that help ensure the long-term integrity and success of the business by caring for their employees and their families. While most mortgage companies regularly and significantly increase the salaries of their top executives, this company keeps large amounts of cash reserves available in case the economy ever softens so they will have funds available to prevent laying off any of their employees." Randy scratched his head. "They know that the decisions they make behind closed doors highly impact their employees. They take very seriously the responsibility that they employ over five thousand people who need to provide for their families. Because of their integrity and genuine care for their employees, the company continues to experience sustained, long-term success."

Randy clapped his hands together triumphantly. "And get this, you would think that because of the large amount of money they have made, their mission statement would include something about hitting sales goals or making a lot of money. That is not the case. One of their core values is to deliver results with integrity. From the top of the organization to the bottom, everyone is striving to live with integrity. It is truly a long-term business advantage."

Matt sat amazed, waiting to hear more of Randy's wisdom.

Chapter 13

Law #3:
Integrity = Your
Best Self

After grabbing some coffee for himself and Matt, Randy sat back down and continued. "Think about the people you see in the news who get exposed for unethical conduct. The aftermath of those highly publicized events is terrible. Not only does the person lose their credibility, but the impact on their personal life, family, and business is usually quite devastating.

Randy took a breath, and had a sip of his coffee. "I heard a story about former baseball manager Tommy Lasorda. He said something to reporters in an interview after a game that really made an impression on me. 'The best day of my life is when I am a manager for this ball club and we win a game, and the second-best day of my life is when I am the manager for this ball club and we lose.'"

"Why would he be happy about losing?" Matt asked.

"He loved what he did. Every single day he went to work, he loved it. He loved the players, his staff, baseball, the fans, and the challenges that came with it. Obviously, as a professional coach, Tommy faced challenges and hardships, just like any leader; but his love of the people and the process was greater than the challenges he faced. Because he had a clear vision of the type of coach and leader he wanted to be, he made the decision to love it all—the good and the bad. Tommy owed it to his coaches, players, and fans to be the best version of himself every day through the ups and downs and difficult decisions—and so do you. . . ."

"That sounds great and all, but I am not playing or coaching in the MLB. I think it would be pretty easy to 'fall in love' with the salaries they bring home if I got to coach or play baseball for a living," said Matt.

Randy smiled. "Living the most satisfying life possible requires being content and planting your feet where you are. Comparison is the thief of joy. You've been greatly blessed and you owe it to the people in your sphere of influence to be the best version of yourself every day, whether you're wiping down tables or running a company, or both. When you live with integrity, you are filled up. When you do the right things the right way and do them with excellence, you feel whole, you are fully content, and you can sleep well at night."

Matt nodded enthusiastically. "It's just such a hard balance. On one hand, I want to always do the right thing, but on the other hand, I want to have financial success. It's almost like I have a battle going on inside me when I make decisions."

Randy smirked. "You are in a battle every day. It's less of a physical battle, though. It's a spiritual one. Here's a verse that helps me to stay grounded. 'For what does it profit a man to gain the whole world and forfeit his soul?' As a leader who is pursuing success, you need to remember that if you make all of the money in the world and have success in the short term, but you lose your principles and everything that's important to you, you will ultimately fail. If you sacrifice your integrity to win today, you will lose in the end. And remember, the more success and power you have, the easier it is to believe that the rules don't apply to you. Abraham Lincoln said it like this: 'Nearly all men can stand adversity, but if you want to test a man's character, give him power.'"

Matt thought about the power he had at work, and how much power he could amass if he made the sale. Some of the co-workers he mistreated at work ran through his mind.

He also thought about how he had seen other people get promoted, then become completely self-centered. He didn't want that for himself. He didn't want to be like Tony.

"So would you say that fighting these battles and staying humble are the secrets to acting with integrity?" Matt asked.

"That's one way to think about it. Something to keep in mind is that when you're living without integrity, you tend to be very self-centered." Randy took a sip of his coffee. "For a leader, self-care is very important, but living with integrity allows you to shift your focus to others. Think about a personal trainer, for example. Most successful personal trainers I know rise very early in the morning to do their own workout. They discipline their own bodies first, then they're able to coach others and give their best to their clients. If you had a personal trainer who didn't actually work out, you would be quite confused and it would be hard to follow their leadership." Randy nodded. "You owe it to yourself and to the others you lead to be the best version of yourself every single day and to be thankful for what you have instead of focusing on what you don't."

Matt began to recount the blessings he had in his life. He considered his wife, kids, grandpa, a great job—and was even grateful for a brother who challenged him to grow. Now he just had to figure out what to do about Thrive Airlines. While he wanted big success, he didn't want to lose his soul in the process. He felt imprisoned by the situation, but thankfully, Randy was about to help him think about it more clearly.

Chapter 14

Law #4: Integrity Frees You to Live

Randy got straight to the point. "This is one of the more straightforward laws, but it can be the most freeing. The truth is, when you live with integrity, you experience peace and contentment, which provides freedom. You're able to be who you really are, rather than being hyper-focused on maintaining false narratives or remembering lies, which puts you on a hamster wheel you can never get off. Think of it like this. Have you ever juggled before?"

"No," Matt laughed. "I don't think I'd be very good at it."

"Exactly," exclaimed Randy, as he went into his bag and grabbed three juggling balls. "Take lying, for example. When you lie, you lack integrity and create a false narrative. So, if I take one of these balls and throw it in the air. It's easy to maintain throwing it up and down to myself. Here, you try."

Matt picked up one of the juggling balls and threw it up and caught it a couple of times. He said, "Yes, I agree, this is easy."

"Okay, great," said Randy. "You can maintain one lie. Now, how about you lie to someone else about something. Here's another ball. Now throw them up and down and see how easy they are to maintain."

Matt threw them both in the air and caught them, but looked more awkward than the first time. "A little harder," Matt said. "But I can still handle this."

"Okay, if you're so sure of yourself, then here's the third ball. Try this." Matt threw the first two balls up in the air and, as he released the third, he failed to catch the original balls he had thrown. He dropped all three on the floor. Other people in the airport swung their heads around. Matt lowered his head, embarrassed.

Law #4: Integrity Frees You to Live

Randy burst into laughter. Although his cheeks were flushed red, Matt shortly followed. Gasping for air, Randy said, "You see," he started, wiping his eyes, "living without integrity requires maintenance. But when you speak the truth and live the truth, no maintenance is required. When you're congruent in all areas of your life, you can sleep well at night because you know that you are not maintaining a lie—you are simply living the truth. What are some areas in your life where you're juggling, and not living the truth?"

"Well, a couple of things spring to mind." Matt composed his thoughts before speaking. "Sometimes I tell white lies to people at work to try to make myself look more impressive. Even though no one sees the sales reports except for management, I sometimes inflate my sales numbers to make myself sound better around my peers. But, that doesn't really affect anyone, so it's not really a big deal."

Randy gave Matt a stern look. "You're wrong. That affects *you*. Every time you tell a lie, you have to maintain it! And then it requires constant maintenance and energy to remember the lie you told and then to make sure that all future conversations and circumstances support it. Having to continually maintain a lie is exhausting and eventually wears you down."

Matt nodded. He found it difficult to believe something so obvious had eluded his thinking. Randy continued, "When you only focus on short-term results and neglect a long-term perspective, you won't have success over the long haul. Companies and employees who have a long-term vision of where they're headed and have integrity along the way are the ones that usually have the most success. The key is having a foundation for your life."

Randy kept on, "I once heard a parable about two men who each built a house. One man built his house on sand and the other built his on rock. When storms came, the house built on sand was destroyed very quickly, but the house that was built on solid rock stood through violent storms.

"The same goes for you. If you build your life on self-serving principles rather than on a strong foundation of integrity, when opportunities arise for you to cut corners, stretch the truth, tell an outright lie, or act in a dishonorable way, you may take them, eventually causing everything around you to collapse." Randy crushed his empty cardboard coffee cup in his hand to demonstrate. "But if you have a strong foundation"—he put one hand on top of the other on the table—"you can live in freedom, knowing that you are anchored to a stable foundation. You've already made the decision about what type of person you are and want to become. The truth is, once you decide who you are and what you stand for, decision-making gets a whole lot easier. Did you know that experts say it's easier for someone to be one hundred percent committed to something than to be only ninety-eight percent committed?"

"Why is that?" Matt leaned forward.

"Simple. The person who is only ninety-eight percent committed to something has to reevaluate their position and make a new decision each time a tough situation arises. But the person who is one hundred percent committed to certain principles understands that the decision has already been made. For example, think of a bodybuilder. Someone who trains to be in a physique competition has to undergo grueling months of eating a strict diet, working out most days to

101

get their body into prime physical condition. The bodybuilder who is one hundred percent committed to being a great bodybuilder doesn't have to decide when someone asks if they'd like a free ice cream cone. They decline because their vision is set on being great and they are all in on pursuing their goal, while the person who is only ninety-eight percent committed has to make a decision whether they will eat it or not each time it is offered.

"The same goes for you. You have to make a decision about the type of person you want to become. If your plan is to have integrity only when it's convenient for you, you'll constantly fight the battle of whether to do the right thing or not. But let me tell you this, I have counseled many business leaders at this very airport. If you do decide to live your life at work and home with integrity, you'll be able to live in freedom. Instead of trying to maintain your story or trying to save face, you'll be able to freely work, live, and love. In my younger days, I thought rules didn't apply to me and that I had the freedom to do whatever I wanted. As it turned out, I was trapped. When I finally decided to get my life together and started becoming the man I was supposed to be, I had to begin taking ownership of my actions and examine my life choices. Only when I did those things and committed myself a hundred percent to a life of integrity did I experience true freedom. And that's what I want you to have."

"Seriously, thank you so much—meeting you has helped me in so many ways," Matt said quietly.

"I feel like you have more going on." Randy squinted at Matt. "Is there something you're not telling me?"

"How can you tell?"

"You look pale as a ghost," Randy half-laughed. Matt joined in nervously.

"Okay, yeah, I have something I need to tell you. I need your advice on a pretty big decision that I have to make this upcoming week. I have the chance to make the sale of a lifetime at work." Randy tilted his head towards Matt. Matt continued, "This would be the big break I've always wanted. The only problem is that the engines we're selling are not quite up to par as far as testing goes." Matt was shaking slightly.

"What do you mean 'not quite up to par'?" Randy asked directly.

"Well . . . they're not ready to be sold legally yet because of testing issues. They will technically be fine, but we haven't received an 'all clear' rating yet. However, if we don't make this sale, we may lose our biggest customer to another competitor that has just begun producing a similar high-efficiency engine. We were the first company to develop these innovative engines and really need this sale. My boss arranged for the testing reports to be altered, to show that the engines passed, in order for the sale to go through. The engines will eventually pass, but they haven't passed yet." Matt scratched his face, then sighed. He wanted someone to tell him that the sale was a good idea.

"Well, it sounds like you have a pretty tough decision on your hands," Randy said. "I won't try to sway your decision in any way because it's your decision to make, but I will ask you one question. Twenty years from now, when you look back on this situation, what decision will make you most proud? I think if you wrestle with that question, you'll come to your

Law #4: Integrity Frees You to Live

own conclusion about what you should do. A fool thinks only about how his decisions will impact him in the moment, but someone who has wisdom considers the long-term implications of his decisions. Never forget that."

Chapter 15

Thrive Airlines

The day finally came for Matt to meet with representatives from Thrive Airlines. They were a huge company whose cheap flight options and great service were a hit with air travelers. They had experienced a 40 percent increase in revenue from the previous year and were continuously seeking ways to increase profitability. With their focus on fuel-efficient engines, they believed Turnbow Technologies had the perfect product—and matched what they were looking for. This was a perfect partnership.

Matt and Tony were able to meet with the CEO of Thrive Airlines, Jade Morgan, who had helped build Thrive Airlines from the ground up. Matt showed Jade the groundbreaking technology that created the fuel-efficient engines. Many other airlines had told Matt that their new technology wouldn't work, and had expressed concerns that the engines hadn't yet passed regulatory testing. But Jade was different. She really liked the technology and conveyed her interest in acquiring it; but without a passed test, she would not be able to sign off on her company buying the product. Matt wanted to keep this positive momentum going, so he assured Jade that they had the test results and he would send them over to her as soon as possible. Matt felt a twinge of discomfort as he noticed how easily the words had flowed from his mouth, yet he felt energized by the thought of getting the bonus of a lifetime.

When Matt walked into Tony's office after the meeting, he was smiling. "Jade mentioned that they need passed test results before they can make things official. When can you get me the certificate and results?" Matt asked

"It's only a call away," Tony said arrogantly. "I told you my guy will take care of us, and he will."

"Do you really think this will work? Using falsified test results? Don't you think . . ."

Tony interrupted, "It'll work, don't question me. I've been doing this much longer than you have. I'm a closer, and this is what I do. I make deals happen."

Tony stood up, walked straight up to Matt, looked him up and down, then left his office. Matt was surprised that a senior leader like Tony—who had a decent amount of sales success in the past—would consider using false test results. Matt began to feel ashamed that he was even considering being part of it. He thought about what Randy had taught him. On one hand, he wanted to make a decision that would keep him from having any moral regrets later in life, but he also knew that $7 million would change his life completely. He could retire, travel, and spend time with his family, like his older brother. Matt's heart pumped fast at the prospect of having that type of money, but he also felt extreme anxiety about being involved in a scheme like this.

As Matt left Tony's office, Tony's receptionist said that the president of Thrive Airlines was very excited that they reported passing scores and would be flying back in with her engineering team in a few days to witness it for themselves. It usually took weeks before an entire team came to visit for the evaluation of a new technology, but this was such an important deal, it was their number one priority. Matt was proud and nervous all at the same time.

Three days later, Matt arrived at work at 4:30 a.m. Thrive Airlines was due to arrive at 9 a.m., and the team had a lot of preparation to do. Matt sat quietly in his office and thought long and hard about what was happening. He realized he would have to show the members of Thrive Airlines the engines with confidence, knowing that they had yet to pass regulatory tests.

Just as Matt began considering the idea of calling Jerry to let him know what was going on, Tony walked in. "Hey! Let's go downstairs. We need to go over a few things before they get here." Matt followed Tony downstairs and they talked through scenarios. Tony said, "If they ask to see test results today, let them know that we are still waiting on the final document to be sent to us, but that we've been given verbal approval. Just tell them we're still waiting on it."

"Got it," Matt replied. Matt was a natural salesman and his high emotional intelligence helped him finish deals. He could read others like a book and knew how to please the people he was selling to. When the Thrive Airlines team arrived, Matt was prepared. He knew the Turnbow engine inside and out as well as all the other engines in his industry. He was confident that Thrive Airlines would move forward with their new product.

"Welcome to Turnbow!" Matt exclaimed as the Thrive Airlines management team walked into the building. "We are excited you are here!" Matt showed the team around the facility and introduced the engineers from both teams to each other. All the Thrive Airlines employees looked delighted. One of them spoke of their excitement to be the first in the industry to have this technology. It could save them millions if they were the first airline to roll it out effectively.

The team was in the building for more than ten hours that day, performing tests and screenings on the engines. Both the president and the engineers were amazed at the performance of the new engines. As Matt walked the Thrive Airlines team out of the building, Jade turned to Matt and said, "You'll be hearing from me soon."

At 5:30 the following morning, Matt got a call from Jade. He expected to hear from her soon, but not this soon. He picked up his phone and left the bedroom.

"Sorry for the early phone call. Are you awake?" asked Jade.

"I am now," Matt replied in a light tone. "Did your flight make it safely?

"Yes, it did." Jade took in a deep breath as Matt tried hard to conceal his yawn. "I have some great news for you." Matt started to feel sick. Jade said, "Our board has agreed to the two hundred fifty-two million dollar price. We are ready to move forward in getting this deal done!" Matt's stomach dropped.

"That's great news!" Matt replied, almost not wanting it to be true.

"Well, it's a no-brainer for us. We're all excited to be the first airline to implement this. Have your team get all the necessary paperwork ready, and your team can come to Thrive Airlines headquarters next week to sign everything and make it official. Our investors, board, and legal team agreed that as long as we have a copy of passed test results, we can move forward."

"Great!" Matt replied, punching the air. "We'll have all of the paperwork ready by next week."

Jade laughed. "Let's make history!"

Matt couldn't believe what had happened. His heart raced. Sweat poured from his forehead. He stared at the blank wall for a few minutes as thoughts raced through his mind. He had waited for a moment like this his entire career. It was all happening so fast.

Not sure what to do next, Matt woke Kendra and told her the news that he might be closing a really big sale. Kendra was excited for him, but something didn't seem right. "You don't look good," she said. "Are you feeling okay?"

"Yes, I'm terrific," Matt replied. "I'm just tired and this deal is really stressful. There are some decisions I'll have to make that might not be the best, but they'll bring in a lot of money for our family."

Kendra stopped Matt quickly and said, "I don't care about money. I'd rather you be there for the kids. I want you to do the right thing, so you can sleep at night. Please don't make a decision based only on money. I love you." Kendra rolled over and drifted back to sleep. Matt stayed wide awake for the 30 remaining minutes until his alarm went off.

Later that morning, Matt burst into Tony's office.

"Do you like the smell of money?" Tony said, pressing a $20 bill to his nose.

Matt nodded slowly, and sat down.

"Good. Let's go get rich!" Matt was shaking, again. "What's wrong?" Tony wondered. Matt found it difficult to respond.

"I don't know if I can do this deal. I'm having second thoughts." Matt stared at the floor. "What would my grandpa think?"

Tony pulled up a chair next to Matt. "Your grandpa is a businessman. He's had to make tough decisions in order to keep this company afloat." Tony put his large bear paw of a hand on Matt's shoulder. "If you make this deal, your grandpa will be proud of you. After all, you're bringing in a lot of money. This will be huge for your career and for the company."

Matt was stuck. He didn't know what to say. All he could muster was that $7 million was a lot of money.

"Exactly. Now let's do this darn thing!" Tony said.

Matt conceded, and a few hours later his team boarded a plane to head to Thrive Airlines headquarters. During the entire flight, Matt worried about what he should do. He considered his grandpa. What would he think of him? Even though Matt didn't see his grandpa as often as he would like, he couldn't think of a better person to emulate, and he wanted to make him proud. Somewhere deep down, despite the promise of all that money, he knew that his grandpa wouldn't do this. Then Matt thought about his family. Legally, if he were to get caught doing this, he could be in serious trouble. What would that mean for his family? He could be arrested for fraud—for participating in a scheme to falsify testing data—and worse yet, for jeopardizing the lives of the airlines' future passengers. Even worse, what if he made the sale and a plane crashed because of falsified test reports? Matt thought back to all the times he had met with Randy. Randy challenged him to make decisions that he would be proud of 20 years from now. Matt knew that he would not be proud of his actions if he went along with the plan, even if he was set for life financially. As the plane landed, Matt came to a decision.

The Sale

Chapter 16

The Sale

Matt stepped off the plane with his team, breathing heavily and sweating profusely. Never in his life had he been so nervous. He couldn't stop thinking about the fact that if this sale happened, moments later he would make millions of dollars. Matt, Tony, and nine other teammates were welcomed by 17 staff members from Thrive Airlines. They walked into the meeting room. Everyone on both sides of the transaction was excited—except for Matt. When the small talk was over, Jade walked in along with a few of her board members and assistants.

"Great to see you," she said, shaking Matt's hand firmly. "Thanks for coming on such short notice. We are very excited about this deal!"

"Thanks," Matt replied. "We are too." Matt and Tony sat down at a large table across from Jade and a few others from her team. In total, there were 37 people in the room. Matt knew this was going to be the biggest test of his life.

Jade's assistant presented 300 pages of paperwork and Tony began signing documents, one after another, on behalf of the company. After Tony had signed all of the necessary documents, Jade asked for a copy of the passed test report. Matt handed it over and Jade accepted it with a smile. "We are going to revolutionize the industry!" exclaimed Jade. "Now all we need is three signatures from the two of you, and this is a done deal," she said as Matt took a deep breath. "Here is the official pen to sign with. . . ." Matt grabbed the pen with his moist palm.

"Are you okay?" Jade asked.

Matt's heart began to race and he felt like everything was happening in slow motion. "Yes, I'm fine," he blurted. "I need to grab some water."

Matt exited the room and headed straight for the bathroom. He burst through the cubicle door and vomited. Whichever option he chose, he would have to let people down. Matt stood for a second, taking deep breaths. He splashed water on his face and looked at himself in the mirror. After patting himself dry with a paper towel, he left the bathroom and walked back into the meeting. With all eyes on him, Matt sat down and grabbed the pen. The room was dead silent as everyone waited for him to sign.

Matt signed the first document. As he moved on to the second document, he put his pen down and muttered, "I can't do this."

"What do you mean?" Jade asked.

"I just . . ." Matt mumbled, before Jade spoke up.

"Every sales rep dreams of being in your position. You are about to broker one of the biggest deals in the history of the aviation industry."

Tony quickly jumped in, "Matt, you don't look well. Let's talk privately for a second." Tony looked at Jade, who nodded. Tony led Matt out of the room into the hallway. "What on earth do you think you're doing?" Tony asked in a firm whisper. "You are about to make the deal of a lifetime and become rich beyond your wildest dreams. What is wrong with you?!"

Matt shrugged his shoulders. "I just can't do this."

"You listen here." Tony clenched his fist in Matt's face. "If you mess this up, no one is going to forgive you. Your grandfather will be disappointed. You will be letting our entire company down."

"I need to do the right thing," Matt said, heading back to the room. Tony tried to get in his way, but Matt barged past him.

"You're an idiot who's going to make the biggest mistake of his life," Tony said from behind him.

"You know what?" Matt turned around. "My grandpa built this company with integrity. He trusts me. I'm not going to be the one to tarnish his reputation."

"Trusts you? You're in this role because he feels sorry for you. You'll be lucky to have a job at all after losing this deal."

Seething with anger, Matt walked past the meeting room further down the hallway and out the front door. Tony brushed himself down and walked back into the room and tried to keep the Thrive Airlines employees at ease.

"Matt's not feeling well," he announced. "I'll sign the papers for him on behalf of the company."

Jade shook her head. "No, I would like Matt to sign them. He is the sales rep I've worked with from the beginning."

Tony rolled his eyes but accepted Jade's wishes. "I think we're going to need a few more minutes. We'll get this done soon."

"Very well," Jade said, before dismissing her staff.

The Sale

Chapter 17

The Decision

As he walked to his hotel room, Matt felt like he was going to pass out from stress and lack of sleep. At the same time, a huge weight had been lifted off his shoulders. He couldn't believe he just turned down $7 million, but deep down he knew it was the right thing to do. The longer he lay in bed, the more doubt crept in about his decision. Matt's phone was blowing up with calls and texts from Tony, telling him to come downstairs and make the deal. One text read, "What room are you in?" but Matt didn't respond. Instead, he put his head in his pillow and tried to fall asleep, hoping to avoid the stress altogether.

Shortly after falling asleep, another text awakened him. He rolled over and saw a text from Jade: "*Where are you?*" Matt's heart dropped. He was nervous, but he knew he needed to talk with Jade. They had forged a good relationship and Jade trusted him. Matt texted her back and they arranged to meet back in the conference room, alone.

As Matt walked into the room, he saw Jade sitting in the same seat as before. Jade looked confused and frustrated. "Why did you and your team come all the way here if you don't want to sell the technology to us?"

"It's quite complicated," Matt replied.

"Is there another airline offering you more money?" Jade asked defensively.

"That's not it," Matt replied quickly. His lip started quivering, but he controlled it and gave Jade an honest answer. "Here's the situation. While the engines have been performing extremely well, the truth is that we haven't received a final passed test yet. I told you we had, but that wasn't true."

"How is that possible?" Jade looked through the stack of documents in her hand. "I have the certification document in this paperwork."

Matt took the paper from Jade. "Don't waste your time." Matt lowered the paper and swallowed. "The document is false."

Jade nodded with her mouth wide open, barely uttering "What?" in response.

"Listen, I never wanted to proceed with this. Tony demanded that we do it and I didn't have the courage to say no. On top of that, I got caught up in the idea of making such a big commission. My grandpa knew nothing about this and would be shocked if he found out. While I feel confident that the engines would perform well for Thrive Airlines in their current state, I couldn't, with good conscience, sell you these engines when they have not fully passed all of the regulatory testing."

"Wow. I can't believe this. Why didn't you wait to get the actual passed results? Why rush?" Jade asked.

Matt interrupted. "I know. I'm sorry. I should never have let it go this far. I was fearful for my job and I've spent my life dreaming of making a sale of this magnitude, so I let my emotions factor into my decision-making. I allowed personal gain to be a higher priority than doing the right thing. We should have waited for the certified test results, but Tony was adamant we proceed. I caved to the pressure. I can't blame anyone else but myself for what has happened. I am so sorry."

Jade sat there and let Matt's words sink in. "I'm going to be honest." She sucked her bottom lip in, then released it. "You did the right thing. You just potentially saved Thrive

Airlines millions of dollars in future lawsuits and possible malfunctions in our aircrafts. I'm annoyed that you let it go this far, but I thank you for your honesty."

A weight lifted off Matt's shoulders.

"We could sue you, you know," Jade said with a stern voice.

"I know. We would deserve it." Matt lowered his eyes.

Jade added, "Listen. I just want you to know that we're not going to do that, and it's going to take some time for us to figure everything out on our end, but if and when the engine passes, I want to be the first person to hear about it. Deal?"

"Deal." Matt shook her hand and added, "I am very confident that they will pass, and when they do, I'll call you immediately."

Matt went back to his hotel room feeling strangely refreshed. He knew he had made the right decision.

After their conversation, Jade quickly called Jerry.

As Jerry answered the phone, Jade stated, "Because of your grandson, we didn't move forward with the sale."

Jerry almost fell out of his seat. "What happened, what did he do wrong?"

"Nothing. In fact, he just saved us big time. It turns out that Tony forged the signatures on the test results. Your engines haven't yet passed all the regulatory tests."

Jerry was stunned. "What? How is this possible? How did you find out?"

Jade explained how Matt refused to sign the papers. She told him how Tony threatened his job if he didn't move forward. She concluded, "Matt did the right thing. I have never seen someone act like that with so much money on the line."

The Decision

Jerry couldn't believe what he was hearing. He was furious that Tony, a man who had worked for Turnbow for almost a decade, would do something like this. But he was also thankful for his grandson's decision.

Jerry responded somberly, "I'm so sorry, I don't even know where to begin. I will make things right and I can promise you that we will work 24/7 on our end to get the test results, so we can get you those engines."

After Jerry and Jade's call, Jerry had Tony terminated immediately. Jerry then picked up the phone and called Matt.

When Matt answered, Jerry said, "You did the right thing for the sake of our company and I'm so proud of you. Jade called and told me everything. Tony has been terminated. Effective immediately, you are now VP of Sales." He took a deep breath. "I think Thrive Airlines will wait until we have passed all the regulatory tests because of your integrity and transparency. Great work."

Chapter 18

The Vote

When Matt arrived home from the trip, Kendra and both kids were there to greet him. As Kendra walked toward him, she noticed that his demeanor was different than it had been before he left.

"You look happy. Less stressed. It must have been a success then?" Kendra asked.

"I'm a lot less stressed, that's for sure." Matt grinned. He explained the entire situation. Kendra threw her arms around him, and he pulled her in close. "So you're not mad at me for turning down all of that money?"

"Of course not. I have everything I need right here inside this house." Kendra rubbed Matt's back. "Thank you for being a man of integrity."

Two months went by. Matt was happy and performing well at work. He was leaving earlier to spend time with his family and leading his sales team effectively. His family and team at work noticed a change in him, and with each visit to see Randy, his leadership improved. They no longer viewed him as Jerry's spoiled grandson whom they were stuck working with, but instead saw him as someone they respected and wanted to work with. A month later, Matt received a call from one of the lead technicians. "We did it! The engine finally passed!"

Matt's heart raced. He said thank you, hung up, and dialed Jade. After six days of negotiating, the sale went through. Jade admitted to Matt that, at times, her team was tempted to look at different companies to seek similar engines, but because Matt had been so honest, Jade continued to wait, allowing Turnbow time to get the final test results.

The Vote

"I'm more interested in long-term success," Jade stated. "Your actions proved that you are too, and that's why we want to do business with you."

Matt couldn't believe it! At the end of the month, he would receive the biggest commission of his life. Seven million dollars. He had waited so long for this moment and couldn't believe he would actually be able to retire early.

Jerry was so proud of his grandson for doing the right thing and closing the biggest deal in Turnbow's history. The story spread through the company like wildfire and Matt was lauded as the hero of the story because of his courage and integrity. Everyone saw the amazing outcome of the drama that had unfolded and they were inspired by Matt's choice to do the right thing in the midst of all the pressure he faced.

While Matt was riding high, Jerry's health continued to decline at a rapid pace. Everyone started to take notice. His board suggested that they speed up the search to find the next CEO to lead Turnbow into the future. After searching externally for a candidate with no luck, one of Jerry's advisors suggested that the team look internally. Jerry agreed. As a place to start, at their next board meeting Jerry handed each board member a piece of paper. To get a working list of feasible candidates, he asked them to write down their best suggestion for who they thought should be considered for the CEO position. The team took some time to ponder their choices, then Jerry collected all twelve papers. When he read them, he was astonished to see that the same name was written on each piece of paper.

Chapter 19

The New CEO

Chapter 19

The New CEO

A month after Matt received his $7 million bonus in crypto currency, he was more optimistic about the future than ever. He had a sit-down meeting with his team and told them how much he appreciated each of them and how much he had enjoyed working with them over the past few years, but that he had decided to retire early and move into his next season of life. While his team members were sad to see him go, they knew that he wanted to travel and have more freedom. Each of them had a true heartfelt fondness for Matt and sincerely wanted the best for him.

After eating some cake and opening a few gifts from his co-workers, Matt sat alone in his office. He looked around at the pictures on the walls and on his desk that had been collected during his time at this great company. As he started to pack things into cardboard boxes, he heard a knock at the door.

It was Jerry. He looked really ill, and Matt felt a lump form in his throat.

Jerry nodded with pride. "Of all the ways I have seen you grow as a person and as a leader, it's the way you have been leading your family that makes me the most proud. I really couldn't be more proud of you."

"Thanks, Grandpa. I'll be sad to leave this place. A lot of great memories and so many great people," Matt said, fighting back tears.

Jerry smiled. "That's why you can't leave yet."

"Grandpa, you know I love this company but . . ."

Jerry cut Matt off. "Well, I have something to tell you before you start getting too sentimental." Jerry laughed and Matt joined in.

"Okay, go ahead, then."

"Our board of advisors had a vote yesterday and unanimously chose you to be the next CEO of this company. This was not my doing. They voted. They want you. I know that you weren't planning on this being thrown at you, but due to my health, we had to make decisions more quickly. I wanted to tell you right away."

Matt sat stunned.

"Listen, I want you to be the next CEO of this company," Jerry said. "Not just because you're my grandson, but because I can trust you to run it the right way. I've been waiting over a decade to find my replacement and I believe you are the perfect fit. I know you have other plans, so if you decide to turn this down, there are no hard feelings. I want you to do what's best for you, Kendra, and the kids."

Matt was at a crossroads. Did he want to spend the rest of his life on vacation, lying on the beach? Or did he yearn for something more?

Jerry added, "I know this is a lot to take in, but next week is our annual all-company retreat. If you accept, we'll introduce you as the new CEO of Turnbow and you can give your first speech as head of the company."

Matt instantly thought back to his meetings with Randy. *"What decision would I be proud of making twenty years from now?"* Matt thought.

Matt agreed tö think about it. Jerry said he had 24-hours to decide, or they'd be searching for someone else. For all of his grandpa's softness and integrity, he was still a businessman, and this was a decision that needed to be made sooner rather than later. Matt talked it over with Kendra and the kids. This wasn't his decision. It was their decision to make together. If they weren't all in, he wouldn't take it. After a short discussion, they decided it would be a great honor to carry on the legacy and tradition of Jerry's company. They knew that Matt would have to work hard, but they would be intentional about taking family trips and making time for what was most important to them as a family.

"How much golf and lying on the beach can you do anyway?" Kendra joked. "Life is so much better when you're living with a greater purpose."

And so it was unanimous. Matt met with Jerry and told him he would take the job.

Chapter 20

The First Speech

Matt and his family checked into the Naples, Florida, hotel where the all-company retreat was being held. After dropping off their bags and relaxing in their rooms, it was time for the evening session to start.

***

Thousands of Turnbow Technologies employees were attending the event, and there was a buzz in the air. Jerry addressed the crowd, telling them how they had just made the biggest sale in the company's history and how proud all the team members should be of themselves. He didn't thank individuals, but teams of people, everyone from the board of directors and technology leaders to entry-level employees. His words were met with rapturous applause.

Before long, Jerry gave Matt a proper introduction as the new CEO. Matt walked up to the podium, humbled yet proud and confident.

After thanking his grandpa, Matt gave a short but spirit-filled talk as the new CEO. He thanked everyone for accepting him and helping him grow. His new maturity meant that he was ready for the biggest role in the company. After he got off the stage, he hugged Kendra and his kids. "You will always come first," he said. "I promise." Kendra smiled. Matt continued, "I want to be the person you married."

Kendra kissed him. "Actually, you can be better than that." Kendra said. Matt laughed and agreed.

After his kids congratulated him, Matt heard a familiar voice behind him. "Randy?! What are you doing here? How did you know about this? It all happened so fast, I haven't even had a chance to come and see you. I wanted to tell you in person."

"Well, your assistant told your grandpa about our meetings, and it turns out he knows a person or two in the aviation industry," he responded, giving Matt a wink. "He reached out to our airport director and tracked me down. He flew me here tonight and, honestly, I would not have missed this for anything. It's been so great to see you grow into the excellent leader you've become. You've passed this first test with flying colors. Congratulations!"

Matt was on the verge of tears. Having Randy at this pivotal moment in his life delighted him.

Randy continued, "It has been a privilege to see you get this promotion and I am so glad to be part of it. I'm so sorry that I can't stay longer. I have to be back at the airport in the morning for work. It's been amazing seeing you and I can't wait for my first meeting with Turnbow's new CEO!"

"Wait one second. . . . I need to ask my grandpa something."

Jerry was talking with a board member when Matt walked up to him and whispered a question in his ear. Jerry responded with a smile and said, "This is your company now. Moving forward, you make these decisions."

"I guess you're right," Matt replied. He walked back over to Randy and told him, "As the new CEO of this company, I want to run it the right way. But I can't do it alone. How would you like to open a Dillon's Pizza inside Turnbow Technologies? We have a food court, and we have over five thousand employees who could use your positive attitude. You could spend a few days each month here and be my leadership coach. What do you think?"

"We mainly have our restaurants in airports and college towns," Randy stated sternly, then winked. "I'll talk to the owner and see what I can do." And just like that, another Dillon's Pizza location was birthed right inside Turnbow's food court.

Matt knew that if he was going to operate Turnbow with integrity, he needed the right people around him. Integrity is not a one-time decision. It is a lifetime decision. It is a decision you make each day for the rest of your life. And life is a whole lot better when you surround yourself with people who choose to live with integrity, hold you accountable, and support you along the way.

Epilogue

Today, Matt has never felt better. He is more confident, more connected to his family, and in charge of a successful company that operates with integrity at every level. Turnbow Technologies remains one of the top aviation technology companies because of their commitment to doing the right thing. Companies from all over the globe visit Turnbow to observe their culture and take strategies back to their own businesses. Under Matt's visionary leadership, Turnbow Technologies was rated as one of the top companies to work for, as well as one of the fastest growing companies in the country.

When a media outlet recently asked Matt about the secret to his success, he explained, "We are not in the aviation sales industry; we are in the people business. We know that when we operate with integrity, as individuals and as a company, everyone gets better. My grandpa did business that way for over forty years, and we won't stop operating in that fashion anytime soon."

The Four Laws of Integrity

Law #1: Integrity Builds Trust

Law #2: Integrity Allows for Long-Term Success

Law #3: Integrity = Your Best Self

Law #4: Integrity Frees You to Live

Resources for The Sale

If you are interested in a keynote or team workshop based on *The Sale*, visit TheSaleBook.com, email info@jongordon.com, or call 904-285-6842.

Visit TheSaleBook.com for:

- An Action Plan
- Resources to help your team build trust and create success

Visit www.TheSaleTraining.com for team workshops and sales training.

Other Books by Jon Gordon

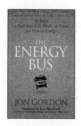

The Energy Bus

A man whose life and career are in shambles learns from a unique bus driver and set of passengers how to overcome adversity. Enjoy an enlightening ride of positive energy that is improving the way leaders lead, employees work, and teams function.

   www.TheEnergyBus.com

The No Complaining Rule

Follow a VP of Human Resources who must save herself and her company from ruin and discover proven principles and an actionable plan to win the battle against individual and organizational negativity.

   www.NoComplainingRule.com

Training Camp

This inspirational story about a small guy with a big heart, and a special coach who guides him on a quest for excellence, reveals the 11 winning habits that separate the best individuals and teams from the rest.

   www.TrainingCamp11.com

The Shark and the Goldfish

Delightfully illustrated, this quick read is packed with tips and strategies on how to respond to challenges beyond your control in order to thrive during waves of change.

   www.SharkandGoldfish.com

Soup

The newly appointed CEO of a popular soup company is brought in to reinvigorate the brand and bring success back to a company that has fallen on hard times. Through her journey, discover the key ingredients to unite, engage, and inspire teams to create a culture of greatness.

www.Soup11.com

The Seed

Go on a quest for the meaning and passion behind work with Josh, an up-and-comer at his company who is disenchanted with his job. Through Josh's cross-country journey, you'll find surprising new sources of wisdom and inspiration in your own business and life.

www.Seed11.com

One Word

One Word is a simple concept that delivers powerful life change! This quick read will inspire you to simplify your life and work by focusing on just one word for this year. *One Word* creates clarity, power, passion, and life-change. When you find your word, live it, and share it, your life will become more rewarding and exciting than ever.

www.getoneword.com

The Positive Dog

We all have two dogs inside of us. One dog is positive, happy, optimistic, and hopeful. The other dog is negative, mad, pessimistic, and fearful. These two dogs often fight inside us, but guess who wins? The one you feed the most. *The Positive Dog* is an inspiring story that not only reveals the strategies and benefits of being positive, but also an essential truth: being positive doesn't just make you better; it makes everyone around you better.

www.feedthepositivedog.com

The Carpenter

The Carpenter is Jon Gordon's most inspiring book yet—filled with powerful lessons and success strategies. Michael wakes up in the hospital with a bandage on his head and fear in his heart after collapsing during a morning jog. When Michael finds out the man who saved his life is a carpenter, he visits him and quickly learns that he is more than just a carpenter; he is also a builder of lives, careers, people, and teams. In this journey, you will learn timeless principles to help you stand out, excel, and make an impact on people and the world.

www.carpenter11.com

The Hard Hat

A true story about Cornell lacrosse player George Boiardi, *The Hard Hat* is an unforgettable book about a selfless, loyal, joyful, hard-working, competitive, and compassionate leader and teammate, the impact he had on his team and program, and the lessons we can learn from him. This inspirational story will teach you how to build a great team and be the best teammate you can be.

www.hardhat21.com

You Win in the Locker Room First

Based on the extraordinary experiences of NFL Coach Mike Smith and leadership expert Jon Gordon, *You Win in the Locker Room First* offers a rare, behind-the-scenes look at one of the most pressure-packed leadership jobs on the planet, and what leaders can learn from these experiences in order to build their own winning teams.

www.wininthelockerroom.com

Life Word

Life Word reveals a simple, powerful tool to help you identify the word that will inspire you to live your best life while leaving your greatest legacy. In the process, you'll discover your why, which will help show you how to live with a renewed sense of power, purpose, and passion.

www.getoneword.com/lifeword

The Power of Positive Leadership

The Power of Positive Leadership is your personal coach for becoming the leader your people deserve. Jon Gordon gathers insights from his bestselling fables to bring you the definitive guide to positive leadership. Difficult times call for leaders who are up to the challenge. Results are the byproduct of your culture, teamwork, vision, talent, innovation, execution, and commitment. This book shows you how to bring it all together to become a powerfully positive leader.

www.powerofpositiveleadership.com

The Power of a Positive Team

In *The Power of a Positive Team*, Jon Gordon draws on his unique team-building experience, as well as conversations with some of the greatest teams in history, to provide an essential framework of proven practices to empower teams to work together more effectively and achieve superior results.

www.PowerOfAPositiveTeam.com

The Coffee Bean

From bestselling author Jon Gordon and rising star Damon West comes *The Coffee Bean*: an illustrated fable that teaches readers how to transform their environment, overcome challenges, and create positive change.

www.coffeebeanbook.com

Stay Positive

Fuel yourself and others with positive energy—inspirational quotes and encouraging messages to live by from bestselling author, Jon Gordon. Keep this little book by your side, read from it each day, and feed your mind, body, and soul with the power of positivity.

www.StayPositiveBook.com

The Garden

The Garden is an enlightening and encouraging fable that helps readers overcome The 5 D's (doubt, distortion, discouragement, distractions, and division) in order to find more peace, focus, connection, and happiness. Jon tells a story of teenage twins who, through the help of a neighbor and his special garden, find ancient wisdom, life-changing lessons, and practical strategies to overcome the fear, anxiety, and stress in their lives.

www.readthegarden.com

Relationship Grit

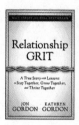

Bestselling author Jon Gordon is back with another life-affirming book. This time, he teams up with Kathryn Gordon, his wife of 23 years, for a look at what it takes to build strong relationships. In *Relationship Grit*, the Gordons reveal what brought them together, what kept them together through difficult times, and what continues to sustain their love and passion for one another to this day.

www.relationshipgritbook.com

Stick Together

From bestselling author Jon Gordon and coauthor Kate Leavell, *Stick Together* delivers a crucial message about the power of belief, ownership, connection, love, inclusion, consistency, and hope. The authors guide individuals and teams on an inspiring journey to show them how to persevere through challenges, overcome obstacles, and create success together.

www.sticktogetherbook.com

The Energy Bus for Kids

The illustrated children's adaptation of the bestselling book *The Energy Bus* tells the story of George, who, with the help of his school bus driver, Joy, learns that if he believes in himself, he'll find the strength to overcome any challenge. His journey teaches kids how to overcome negativity, bullies, and everyday challenges to be their best.

www.EnergyBusKids.com

Thank You and Good Night

Thank You and Good Night is a beautifully illustrated book that shares the heart of gratitude. Jon Gordon takes a little boy and girl on a fun-filled journey from one perfect moonlit night to the next. During their adventurous days and nights, the children explore the people, places, and things they are thankful for.

The Hard Hat for Kids

The Hard Hat for Kids is an illustrated guide to teamwork. Adapted from the bestseller *The Hard Hat*, this uplifting story presents practical insights and life-changing lessons that are immediately applicable to everyday situations, giving kids—and adults—a new outlook on cooperation, friendship, and the selfless nature of true teamwork.

www.HardHatforKids.com

One Word for Kids

If you could choose only one word to help you have your best year ever, what would it be? *Love? Fun? Believe? Brave?* It's probably different for each person. How you find your word is just as important as the word itself. And once you know your word, what do you do with it? In *One Word for Kids,* bestselling author Jon Gordon—along with coauthors Dan Britton and Jimmy Page—asks these questions to children and adults of all ages, teaching an important life lesson in the process.

www.getoneword.com/kids

Other Books by Jon Gordon

The Coffee Bean for Kids

From the bestselling authors of *The Coffee Bean,* inspire and encourage children with this transformative tale of personal strength. Perfect for parents, teachers, and children who wish to overcome negativity and challenging situations, *The Coffee Bean for Kids* teaches readers about the potential that each one of us has to lead, influence, and make a positive impact on others and the world.

www.coffeebeankidsbook.com

Other Books by Jon Gordon

Also by Alex Demczak

ALEX DEMCZAK

Thrive U is a hard-hitting sports devotional that inspires athletes to Thrive! One hundred collegiate and professional athletes representing 20 sports from across the country document their testimonies, trials, and triumphs as they aim to play for a bigger purpose.